First Steps
in Basic Fortran

I. Menai Gentoy.

First Steps in Basic Fortran

L. J. Slater

Department of Applied Economics,
University of Cambridge

CHAPMAN AND HALL LTD

11 NEW FETTER LANE, LONDON EC4

First published 1971
© 1971 *Lucy J. Slater*
Printed in Great Britain by
Butler & Tanner Ltd, Frome and London

SBN 412 10120 3

Distributed in the U.S.A.
by Barnes & Noble, Inc.

Preface

This book is intended to provide a simple introduction to the language of computer programming called Fortran. The work is addressed to teachers, sixth form pupils and students in technical schools and universities whose basic training has been in subjects such as Economics or Sociology, rather than in the traditional scientific subjects of Physics and Mathematics. For this reason, the examples and exercises are drawn mainly from the field of elementary statistics, and no mathematical knowledge is assumed beyond a little basic algebra.

The main parts of a computing system are explained together with the concept of flow charts for working out the steps in a program. Chapters cover the rules governing algebraic statements and simple input and output lists in Fortran. The elements of the language are developed up to two-dimensional arrays and the rules governing simple functions and subroutines. The work ends with a program to carry out an elementary regression analysis.

GOTO is one word in POP2 and GO TO is 2 words in FORTRAN

Contents

Preface   v

1 The main parts of a computing system

1.1 Introduction   1
1.2 The main store   1
1.3 The accumulators   2
1.4 The multipliers   4
1.5 The input and the output   6
1.6 Auxiliary stores   8
1.7 The main parts of a programming system   9
1.8 The organizing program   10
1.9 Compilers   10
1.10 The concept of control in a program   11
1.11 The flow chart   12
1.12 Types of orders in a program   14

2 The arithmetic statement

2.1 Definition   17
2.2 Addition   18
2.3 Subtraction   19
2.4 Multiplication   20
2.5 Division   21
2.6 Brackets   22
2.7 Programming forms   24
2.8 Integers   25
2.9 Exponentation   28

3 The logical statement

3.1 Labels   30
3.2 The 'If' order   32
3.3 The simple loop   33
3.4 An example on a simple survey   37

4 Input and output

4.1 Read and write orders 41
4.2 Simple lists 45
4.3 Integer formats 47
4.4 Heading and terminating sequences 49
4.5 How to get your program running 52
4.6 The H format 56
4.7 The A format 58
4.8 The continuation symbol 59

5 Loops and subscripted variables

5.1 Counting in a cycle 62
5.2 Subscripted variables 64
5.3 The 'dimension' statement 65
5.4 'Do' loops 68
5.5 Nested 'Do' loops 75
5.6 Named variables 82
5.7 Real and integer statements 83
5.8 Arrays 84

6 Functions and subroutines

6.1 Built-in functions 88
6.2 General functions 91
6.3 Subroutines 95
6.4 An example of a simple regression program 96

Further reading

102

Index

102

1 The main parts of a computing system

1.1 Introduction

Consider
$$A = 1 \cdot 5$$
$$B = 2 \cdot 1$$
$$C = A + B$$

These are three orders from a computer program. If you have enough knowledge of algebra to know what the value of C is when these three orders have been obeyed, then you have enough knowledge of mathematics to become a computer programmer. Just as it is not necessary to understand the workings of the internal combustion engine in order to drive a car, so it is not necessary to know anything about electronics in order to make intelligent use of an electronic computer. The user needs only to know a few simple facts about the main parts of a computing system in order to use it.

There are seven main components of a computing system:

(1) the main store
(2) the accumulators
(3) the multipliers
(4) the input system
(5) the output system
(6) the power supplies
(7) the auxiliary storage units

1.2 The main store

An electronic computer consists of a number of cabinets, each packed with electronic equipment.

One or two of these cabinets will contain the main storage units.

These cabinets, when opened, will be seen to contain a large number of identical units, each one of which is capable of holding a pattern of electrical impulses. One pattern of electrical impulses represents one number or one instruction within the computer. A very small modern computer will have 1024 such units to form its main store. The number 1024 is a power of 2, $1024 = 2^{10}$. It is the basic unit for measuring the size of a computer. We say that a computer with 1024 stores has a store of size 'one K'. A very large computer will have as many as $256K$ storage units, that is over a quarter of a million stores. Each store is physically very small however. Often it consists of a printed circuit no bigger than a postage stamp.

Our small computer with $1K$ stores can be thought of as a row of 1024 pigeon-holes. Each such box can hold at a given moment one number or one instruction. A simple teaching machine to simulate the action of a computer can consist of 26 small boxes, with the names A, B, C, . . ., Z, respectively. Each box contains a slip of paper on which one instruction or number can be written.

1.3 The accumulators

The accumulator is a special type of storage unit. The computer can copy one number from any store in the computer into the accumulator, add, or subtract, any other number from any store in the computer and then leave the result of the addition or subtraction in the accumulator ready to be copied into any store in the computer.

Suppose that the number 936·0 is stored in the location called A. We shall write this as

$$A = 936·0$$

that is, the contents of the storage location called A equal 936·0. Then the problem of bringing this number 936·0 from its storage location A into the main accumulator, can be thought of as the act of looking at the slip of paper in the box called A and copying the contents, namely 936·0, onto a new slip of paper, called the accumulator. The original slip, with the number 936·0 upon it, is left unchanged in the box called A. We can write this as

$$C(Acc) = A = 936·0$$

Now let us suppose that a second number, say 211·0, is stored in the box called B, so that

$$B = 211·0$$

This number 211·0 can now be added to the contents of the accumulator, that is to 936·0, and the result can be stored in another location, say in the location called C. We do not have to work out all these steps. We simply give the computer the order $C = A + B$.

Let us place ourselves in the position of the computer for a moment. We have to read the 'add' order, represented by the addition symbol $+$, look at the slip of paper in box B and add the number we find there, 211·0, into our accumulator, so that now

$$C(Acc) = A + B$$
$$= 936·0 + 211·0$$

Next we perform the addition and find the result 1147·0 is in the accumulator, that is

$$C(Acc) = 1147·0$$

We can now copy this result onto a new slip of paper which we store in the box named C, so that

$$C = 1147·0$$

In a similar way, the accumulator can be used to perform subtraction.

Most modern computing systems have what is known as a floating point package. This is a built-in set of orders which enables the machine to handle positive or negative decimal numbers over a very wide range of values whilst keeping the decimal point in the correct position.

Example 1.1

Suppose that:
$$A = 101·72$$
$$B = 1105·31$$
$$C = 0·05$$

We want to form $101·72 - 1105·31 + 0·05$ in the store called D.

The order in our program is $D = A - B + C$. The actual steps in our program might be:

$$C(Acc) = A$$
$$C(Acc) = A - B$$
$$C(Acc) = C(Acc) + C$$
$$D \quad\; = C(Acc)$$

and the computer positions the decimal point automatically. The contents of stores A, B and C remain unaltered, but the contents of the accumulator change at each step in the program. It should be noted that each step in the calculation has to be carried out before the next step is started, and even in such a simple calculation there are many steps involved. Hence we can see why computers have to be not only large but also very fast in their operation.

There is one other function carried out by the accumulator. It has a device upon it to test the sign of a number, and to direct the computer to carry out different sequences of operations according to whether the value of the number is positive, zero or negative. With this simple device the computer changes from a mere calculating machine into a proper automatic computer, capable of carrying out a long series of operations, and of taking decisions as to the correct course to follow when offered a number of alternatives.

1.4 The multipliers

In order to perform multiplication or division it is necessary to have another special type of unit in the computer, known as a multiplier.

Example 1.2

Suppose that $A = 70.2$, $B = 71.5$ and $C = 0.073$. We shall indicate a multiplier by M and the multiplication by the symbol $*$. The order to give the result of $70.1 * 71.5 * 0.073$ might be $D = A * B * C$. The actual steps in carrying out this order are:

$$C(Acc) = A$$
$$C(M) \;\; = B$$
$$C(Acc) = C(Acc) * C(M) \quad (= A * B)$$

$$C(M) = C$$
$$C(Acc) = C(Acc) * C(M) \quad (= (A * B) * C)$$
$$D = C(Acc)$$

Let us sum up the relationships between the main three types of unit in a computer by means of a diagram showing how numbers, or orders, can be transferred from one part of the computer

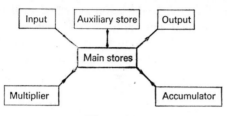

Figure 1.1

to another part. Such a diagram is called a flow diagram because it shows the flow of information from one place to another within the computer.

Exercises 1.1

Write out the steps needed in a program to evaluate

1 $51\cdot3 + 17\cdot1 * 3\cdot4$
2 $(51\cdot3 + 17\cdot1) * 3\cdot4$
3 $(7\cdot1 - 5\cdot2)/(7\cdot1 + 5\cdot2)$

In exercise **3**, there are three parts to the program. First we need to work out the value of $(7\cdot1 - 5\cdot2)$ and store it. Then we need to work out the value of $(7\cdot1 + 5\cdot2)$ and store it. Finally we need to carry out the division.

If we had to work out such a sequence of orders afresh for each calculation it would be quicker to carry it out by hand. However, the same sequence or orders which evaluated $(7\cdot1 - 5\cdot2)/(7\cdot1 + 5\cdot2)$ will also evaluate $(3\cdot7 - 2\cdot1)/(3\cdot7 + 2\cdot1)$. In general if we use the symbol $(x - y)/(x + y)$ to show the structure, the same sequence of orders can be used to work out $(x - y)/(x + y)$ for any values of x and y.

1.5 The input and the output

Every computing system has to have some means of receiving information into the main store from the outside world. This is called its input, and in some ways it is equivalent to the eyes of the human being when he reads information from his computing sheet before he starts to do a calculation. The two most usual input devices are paper tape readers and punched card readers. Both these devices depend on photo-electric cells which sense the presence or absence of a hole in the paper tape, or punched card, which is being read. The computer's readers convert the patterns

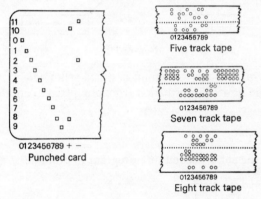

Figure 1.2

of holes into similar patterns of electronic impulses, which are then transmitted to their correct places in the main store. The information being input may be in the form of either numbers, that is the data required for the calculations, or orders, that is the instructions on how to carry out the calculations.

Both types of information can be coded into patterns of holes either on the paper teleprinter tape, or on the punched cards. Paper tape comes in three sizes, 5 track, containing 5 tracks into which holes can be punched, 7 track and 8 track. Each tape has a small set of equally spaced holes running between the third and fourth tracks. These are called the sprocket holes. Each hole is sensed by a photo-electric cell in the reader as the tape is passed at high speed under the reading head. It is most important that all the holes be cleanly cut and evenly spaced or the reader will not read the tape accurately.

The 5 track tape is the oldest type of tape. It is ordinary ticker tape and is restricted by its five tracks to the 32 symbols consisting of most of the capital letters of the alphabet and the ten digits 0 to 9. The wider tapes have 7 tracks with 128 possible symbols and 8 tracks with 256 possible symbols, so that they can give a wider range of information to the readers.

Punched cards are cards similar in size and thickness to post-cards. Each card has on it 80 columns and each column can contain up to three holes in any of 12 possible positions. This gives 77 possible symbols, including all the capital letters, the digits 0 to 9 and some other symbols, such as brackets.

Any small computer must have at least one tape reader or card reader for input, but a large computing system will have several input devices of each type, as well as a typewriter for direct input of small quantities of information or single orders.

All the orders for a calculation have to be input into the main store of the computer, as well as the actual data needed for the calculation, before any calculation can start.

Every computer must have some means of presenting its answers to the outside world. The most usual device for a small computer is a lineprinter. This prints the results one line at a time onto rolls of paper. Tape punches to punch out answers onto paper tape and card punches to punch out results onto cards are also quite usual in the larger computing systems.

Here is an example of lineprinter output from a computer.

```
CYCLE NO. 5
A = 1·3251  B = −1·3398  C = 0·0131
D = 1·23E−5  X = −5·34E 6
END
```

The pattern or format of this output is determined by the program within the computer and is decided by the programmer. We should note that the programmer has made the program to output some text as well as the actual numerical answers. Here the words CYCLE NO. and END, the symbols A = B = C = D = E = and various spaces and new lines have been printed

to help people to identify the various results. The program also
has to be made to output each answer in its correct format. Thus
here the cycle number is printed as a single digit integer without
a decimal point. The three answers A, B and C are printed with
their correct signs in a fixed pattern, with one figure before the
decimal point and four figures after it. In the case of answer C,
this means that only three significant digits are printed, since C is
small. The results D and X are printed in 'floating point', since D
is very small and X is very large, to avoid the loss of significant
figures. The digits following the letter E in each result, represent
powers of ten, so that the true values of D and X are

$$D = 0{\cdot}0000123 \quad \text{and} \quad X = -5340000{\cdot}0$$

Here D and X are both printed to three significant figures,
although one is very small and the other is very large.

1.6 Auxiliary stores

The main store of a computer is often not large enough to contain
all the information, orders and numbers, needed to carry out a
large calculation. So most computing systems have some sort of
auxiliary storage system. The main store of a computer has random
access, that is, it is just as easy to put information into, or take
information out of, any storage location whatever its position in
the store of the computer. Most types of auxiliary store have the
drawback that the information is arranged in sequence, so that it
has to be read into the auxiliary store in sequence, and can only
be taken out of the auxiliary store in the same sequence.

The usual auxiliary store consists of two or more magnetic tape
units. These are machines capable of storing information on
magnetic tape similar to that used in ordinary tape recorders. The
information to be written onto the tape is read from the main store,
in strict sequence. When we want to read it back into the main
store, if the information that we want to read is at the far end of
the magnetic tape, much time can be wasted in positioning the reel
of tape, so that the actual information which we want is brought
into the correct position under the reading head of the tape unit.

Other types of auxiliary store are magnetic disc files, which are similar in use to magnetic tape units but are larger and faster in operation, and magnetic card files, which store information on cards of magnetic material, just as information is stored on ordinary punched cards.

1.7 The main parts of a programming system

Up to now we have only considered single orders and numbers stored within the computer. The entire sequence of orders needed by the computer to carry out the calculation is called the program. The sequence of numbers and other information needed to carry out the calculations is called the data.

The actual physical units of the computer are called the 'hardware'. These are the items already described. Supplied by the computer manufacturer, along with the hardware are a number of ready-made programs, called 'systems' programs. These carry out such necessary tasks as reading the input, printing the results and generally organizing the calculations. These ready-made programs are called the 'software' of the system. Usually, in any computing system, more than 50% of the total cost of the system is represented by the cost of developing these software programs. This ratio, of cost of programs to cost of actual machinery, is increasing with every new generation of computers, as the rate of hardware development slows down and the rate of software development speeds up. These systems programs are usually kept on magnetic tapes ready for use with the smaller computing systems, or on disc files, or in a special part of the main store in the larger systems. Master copies are also kept on paper tape or cards, in case the magnetic tape becomes damaged. The systems programs provided with a computer usually consist of an organizing program, also known as the operating system or executive system, and one or more compiling programs. Each program is built up from a number of separate sections called 'sub-programs' or 'subroutines'.

1.8 The organizing program

This consists of a number of sub-programs which carry out such tasks as controlling the input and output of the system, controlling any magnetic tape units or other peripheral machines, which may be joined to the computer, and checking the time used by each user. They also perform a set of standard engineering checks when the computer is first switched on, to seek any faults in the hardware systems. When such a fault is detected, they print warning information for the engineers, to help them to locate the faults.

Most large computing systems are able to carry out the calculations required by several programs at one and the same time. Such systems are called 'time-shared' systems. The organizing program in such a system will allocate various sections of the store to each separate program, and the necessary input and output devices for each separate program. It will also arrange a system of priorities, so that every program can be carried out as quickly as possible and the computer can make the most efficient use of any facility in short supply.

1.9 Compilers

Every type of computer has what is known as a basic machine code. This consists of elementary orders which are held in the store of the computer, as patterns of electronic impulses, in the same way as numbers are held in the store. Thus, in a typical basic machine code, the order 12 191 would mean 'add the contents of store number 191 into the accumulator . Here the number 12 is stored as an ordinary number within the computer, but is obeyed as the order 'add'. If the computer encounters the number 12 in a storage location where it is expecting to find an item of data, it will treat 12 as a number, but if it finds the same pattern of electronic impulses representing the number 12 in a storage location where it is expecting to find an order, it will obey the pattern as the order 'add'. All the early programs had to be written in a basic machine code, but as every different type of computer has its own basic code, it is very difficult and tedious to have to translate a program from one basic machine code to another one. Since a large part of the cost of a computing system is in the development of programs, such translation is very wasteful of both time and human brain power. Hence what are known as 'source program' languages have been developed. These languages enable a program written for one computing system to be run on a different system, with little or no alteration.

The special program, kept within the computing system to translate a program from a source language into the correct basic machine code language, is called a 'compiler'.

The two main source languages used by modern computers are Fortran and Algol. Fortran (Formula translator) was developed in the first place by the IBM company to make the writing of computer programs of a scientific type easier. It has found world-wide approval and is the main source language used in most scientific computing laboratories. Algol was developed as an ideal programming language. The compilers which translate from Algol to basic machine code tend to be much larger and more wasteful of machine time than the corresponding Fortran compilers, and for this reason Algol is not favoured as a practical computing language, although it is used often in printed literature on programming as it has a good logical structure.

The simplest version of Fortran in common use is called basic Fortran. Compilers for basic Fortran contain all the facilities described in this work. ASA Fortran is a version of the language which contains many extra facilities as well as all the facilities of basic Fortran. PL/1 is the fullest source language of all. It contains even wider facilities than ASA Fortran or Algol.

1.10 The concept of control in a program

The point in the program at which the computer is actually carrying out an order at a given moment is said to be the point reached by the 'control' in the program. Thus we can say that the computer 'sends control' to the first order in the program sequence. Normally, control passes from the first order to the second order in the program, from the second order to the third order in sequence and so on until it reaches the last order in the program. Then control is handed back from the program to the organizing program of the computing system.

There are special types of orders which may occur anywhere in a program, called 'jump' orders. These jump orders cause the machine to obey program orders out of their natural sequence. Thus control may pass in sequence from order number 1 through orders 2 to 9, to order 10. If order 10 is a jump order, for example:

Go back to order 2 if C(Acc) is greater than 0,

this jump order will cause control to go back to order 2, if the test is satisfied, and to obey again the orders numbered 2 to 9 many times over until the test

$$C(Acc) > 0$$

is not satisfied. Then, and only then, will control be allowed to pass on to the next order, order 11. The diagram of the flow of control in this simple program might be drawn thus:

Example 1.3

Enter from the main organizing program to start obeying the program at

> order number 1
> order 2
> order 3
> . . .
> order 10, the test order, jump back to order number 2 if
> $C(Acc) > 0$
> order 11, reached only if $C(Acc) \leqslant 0$
> order 12
> . . .

and so on to the stop order, when control goes back to the organizing program.

1.11 The flow chart

Diagrams like the one above, which show the flow of control in a program, are called flow charts or flow diagrams. They are an aid to the human programmer in working out the logical structure of the proposed program. The flow chart should always be worked out and drawn up for every new program, before the actual detailed writing out of orders is attempted. There are certain conventions used in drawing up flow charts.

Arrows and flowlines such as → ↑ ← ↓ show the direction of the logical flow of the calculation.

Oblong boxes   contain   simple   calculation instructions.

Boxes with rounded ends   are   used   for   input and output orders.

DECISION

Diamond-shaped boxes ◇ are used for orders which

imply a test, so that control takes a different path according to the result of the test.

A number in brackets, for example (9), is used to join one section of a program to another, and to indicate entry and exit points. Templates can be bought quite cheaply to enable programmers to draw their flow charts out neatly. To simplify the task of the printer, the flow charts in this work will only show the distinctive ends of the three types of box, [ ], ( ) or ⟨ ⟩.

Example 1.4 *on flow charts*

A child has to be taught to cross the road in safety. The flow chart for the process might be something like the diagram shown on p. 14.

Unfortunately, when the child was told to cross the road, obeying these orders exactly, he just stood on the pavement alternately looking and waiting indefinitely. You see there was a parked

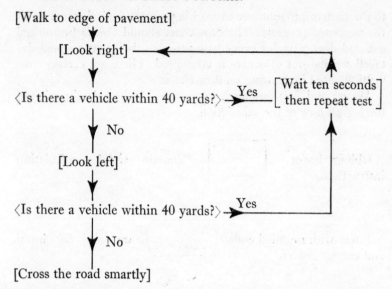

[Cross the road smartly]

vehicle in the street within 40 yards, so both the text orders had to be altered to

⟨Is there a vehicle moving towards you within 40 yards?⟩

Then the child crossed easily in safety. This illustrates the need to design flow charts carefully and to frame the orders needed accurately and exactly.

1.12 Types of orders in a program

We have seen that there are three types of boxes used in a flow chart. These correspond to the three main types of orders used in a program. These are:

(*i*) *Arithmetical statement.* These do the arithmetic type of operation and are shown by the boxes with square ends: for example,

```
Add A to B
```

(*ii*) *The input and output statements.* These are shown in boxes with round ends, and carry out all the operations concerned with getting information into the computer and results out of the computer; for example,

Read the next number and set A equal to it

(*iii*) *Logical statements.* These control the logical flow of the sequence of orders in a program. They are branching types of operation and show the points in the program at which the path of control can take two or more different ways, according to the choice made. They occupy boxes with diamond-shaped ends and they always have one entry point for control and two or at most three alternative paths for the control to pass from them; for example,

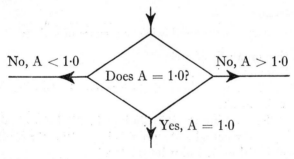

No, A < 1·0   Does A = 1·0?   No, A > 1·0

Yes, A = 1·0

Example 1.5

Suppose that we have a data tape consisting of groups of positive numbers and every group ends with a negative number −1·0. We want to find the sums of the items in each group not counting the −1·0. The flow diagram would look something like the diagram on p. 16.

The difficulty here is that we do not know in advance how many numbers there are in any one group of data, and every group can have a different number of items. Here −1·0 is used as a signal that the end of one group has been reached and 0·0 is used as a signal that the end of all the data has been reached.

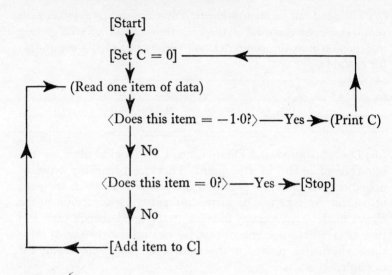

Exercises 1.2

Draw flow charts for the following sequences of actions.

1   Putting on a pair of socks.
2   Boiling an egg.
3   Form the sum of the first 20 integers, in location A, and
     print the result.
4   Read the total income initially into B. Find the tax payable
     at 40p in the pound and store this in A. Print the result.
5   Form 1/10! in A, and print the result.
     Note: 10! means $1 \times 2 \times 3 \times 4 \times 5 \times 6 \times 7 \times 8 \times 9 \times 10$.

2 The arithmetic statement

2.1 Definition

Consider again:

$$A = 1{\cdot}5$$
$$B = 2{\cdot}1$$
$$C = A + B$$

These three lines are examples of the type of order called an arithmetic statement. Each such order occupies one line in the hand-written version of a computer program, and this line is intended to define the value of the item which occurs first in the line. Thus the statement

$$A = 1{\cdot}5$$

sets the item identified by the letter A equal to the numerical quantity 1·5. It would be wrong to write the statement the other way round, thus

$$1{\cdot}5 = A$$

as the Fortran compiler would interpret this statement as an order to set the known quantity 1·5 equal to the unknown quantity A.

The item being defined must always stand by itself as the first item on the line and it must always be followed immediately by the equals sign, =. There must not be more than one equals sign in one line. The expression after the equals sign must consist of an algebraic expression made up only from the items which have been defined in previous parts of the program, symbols such as + or −, the brackets (and), and ordinary numbers.

Just as the order of items in a line is important, so is the sequence of lines in a program. It would be wrong to write the above orders in the sequence:

$$A = 1 \cdot 5$$
$$C = A + B$$
$$B = 2 \cdot 1$$

Here, at the second line $C = A + B$, the compiler would either not have any value defined for the quantity B or it would take some earlier value that B had assumed, and not the required value $2 \cdot 1$.

We must beware of the fact that an arithmetic order is not the same thing as an algebraic equation. After the order has been obeyed by the computer, the item on the left has been given the value that the statement on the right had before the order was carried out. Thus it is perfectly correct to write two orders

$$A = 1 \cdot 5$$
$$A = A + 1 \cdot 0$$

Before the second order is obeyed, A has the value $1 \cdot 5$, but after the second order has been carried out, A has the value $2 \cdot 5$.

2.2 Addition

In the first place, we shall use only the capital letters A, B, – – –, G, H and Ō, P, – – –, Y, Z for the items in a program and ordinary positive decimal numbers. The arithmetic symbol + (plus), the addition sign, will mean addition.

Examples 2.1

Say what is wrong with these programs.

1     $E = 30 \cdot 0$
       $F = 21 \cdot 0$
       $G = E + D$

      Here D has not been defined when it occurs on the right-hand side of the last line.

2     $A = 35 \cdot 1$
       $B = 22 \cdot 2$
       $C + 3 \cdot 0 = A + B$

Here C + 3·0 is not a single undefined item, when it occurs on the left-hand side of the last line.

3   D = 13·75 + 21·30
E = 30·21 + G + 15·72
F = E + D

Here G is not defined when it occurs in the second line.

Now we are in a position to write simple little programs for ourselves.

4   Write a program to find the sum of 3·75, 2·11, 1·93 and 1·38. Our program might be:

$$A = 3·75$$
$$B = 2·11$$
$$C = 1·93$$
$$D = 1·38$$
$$E = A + B + C + D$$

At the end of this sequence of orders, the item E would have the required value.

Exercises 2.1

1   Write a program to form the sum of the 6 items 1·51, 1·75, 2·11, 2·32, 2·72 and 3·1.

2   Write a program to form the sum of the three sides of a triangle 1·5, 2·3 and 3·1.

2.3 Subtraction

We shall use the sign — (minus) for subtraction. Thus we might have in our program the sequence of orders:

$$A = 3·75$$
$$B = 2·11$$
$$C = A - B$$

Also we assume now that our letters A to H and Ō to Z can assume negative decimal values as well as positive ones. Thus we can write:

$$A = 3·75$$
$$B = 2·11$$
$$C = B - A$$

Here the final value of C is −1·64.

We cannot have two arithmetic symbols occurring next to one another in a program. Thus it is wrong to write:

$$A = 3 \cdot 75$$
$$B = 2 \cdot 11$$
$$C = B + -A$$

but we can write:

$$A = 3 \cdot 75$$
$$B = 2 \cdot 11$$
$$C = -A + B$$

that is to say, the + or − signs can occur next to the = sign in a line of program.

Exercise 2.2

What is wrong with the program:

$$A = 13 \cdot 52 = B$$
$$C = -B + A + 2 \cdot 12$$
$$D = -C$$
$$E = D - +C$$
$$F + E = C?$$

Write out a program to do the same thing correctly.

In the first line, there are two = signs. In the fourth line, a + follows immediately on a − sign, and in the last line, the left-hand side of the statement is not a single quantity.

2.4 Multiplication

We shall use the sign * (asterisk), as the arithmetic symbol for the process of multiplication. We do not use the sign × as it might be mistaken for the letter X. Thus:

$$A = 12 \cdot 0$$
$$B = 10 \cdot 0$$
$$C = A * B$$

would set C to the value 120·0.

Example 2.2

Write a program to find the sum of the areas of three rectangles, of sides 1,2, 2,3 and 3,4 inches long respectively. The program might be:

$$A = 1 \cdot 0$$
$$B = 2 \cdot 0$$
$$C = A * B$$
$$D = 3 \cdot 0$$
$$E = B * D$$
$$F = 4 \cdot 0$$
$$G = D * F$$
$$H = C + E + G$$

At this point, H has the value of the sum of the three rectangles.

Exercises 2.3

1 Write a program to find the volume of a cube with sides 2 units long.
2 Write a program to find the volume of a rectangular block with sides 3, 4 and 5 units long respectively.

2.5 Division

The symbol for division is /, the solidus. We shall not use ÷ for division, as this sign does not occur in most computer languages.

Example 2.3

Write a program to evaluate

$$3 \cdot 75 \times 2 \cdot 11 \div 1 \cdot 93$$

Our program might be:

$$A = 3 \cdot 75$$
$$B = 2 \cdot 11$$
$$C = A * B$$
$$D = 1 \cdot 93$$
$$E = C/D$$

Then E has the value of the expression above.

We must never ask the computer to divide by zero, and we shall see later how to insert tests in our programs to guard against this fault. All divisions must always be checked carefully to make sure that they cannot imply division by zero.

Example 2.4

What is wrong with this program?

$$A = 13{\cdot}52$$
$$B = 10{\cdot}01$$
$$B = B + 3{\cdot}51$$
$$C = A - B$$
$$D = B/C$$

2.6 Brackets

We have seen that we must not write one arithmetic operator +, −, * or / immediately following another one. Thus we cannot write

$$C = A + -B$$

However, we can insert round brackets in an arithmetic expression, just as we do in ordinary algebra. Thus, we can write

$$A = C + (-B)$$

Similarly, we might write

$$A = (B + C)/D$$

We must always be most careful, when we are doing a division, to insert round brackets, to make it absolutely clear which is the divisor, and which is the dividend. Thus the program:

$$B = 1{\cdot}0$$
$$C = 4{\cdot}0$$
$$D = 2{\cdot}0$$
$$A = B + C/D$$

would mean to the computer that A takes the value of B added to (C divided by D), that is $A = 1{\cdot}0 + (4{\cdot}0/2{\cdot}0) = 3{\cdot}0$. But the program:

$$B = 1{\cdot}0$$
$$C = 4{\cdot}0$$
$$D = 2{\cdot}0$$
$$A = (B + C)/D$$

gives to A the value $(1{\cdot}0 + 4{\cdot}0)/2{\cdot}0 = 2{\cdot}5$.

In the elementary form of Fortran that we are studying here, we are allowed to use only the round opening bracket, (, and the round closing bracket,). Each opening bracket must be matched in the same line by a closing bracket. We are not allowed to use the square brackets [and] nor the cursive brackets { and }. We can have as many pairs of brackets in one expression as we like, for example

$$A = ((B + C)/(D - (E + F)))/(G + 3{\cdot}0)$$

When we are checking that we have written a complicated order like this one correctly, it is a useful trick to count that the number of left-hand brackets, (, is equal to the number of right-hand brackets,). In this example there are five of each.

Expressions containing brackets are evaluated from the innermost brackets outwards. Thus in the above expression, E + F would be formed first, being at the third depth of brackets, the expressions at the second depth B + C and D - (E + F) would be formed next, and then the expressions at the first depth of brackets, that is the division (B + C)/(D - (E + F)) and the addition G + 3·0 would be carried out. Finally the calculation outside all the brackets would be done, in this case, the last division by (G + 3·0).

In an expression involving addition, subtraction, multiplication and division, the multiplications and divisions are carried out first by the Fortran compiler, and then the additions and subtractions. Thus

$$F = A * B + C/D$$

would mean the result of A times B added to the result of dividing C by D. It is always better to include brackets in such expressions and so avoid any possibility of ambiguity. Thus it is better to write the above statement in the form

$$F = (A * B) + (C/D)$$

Exercises 2.4

1   Write programs to evaluate

$(21\cdot3 + 15\cdot7)/2\cdot9$,
$(13\cdot5 - 21\cdot3)/(31\cdot5 + 7\cdot1)$,
$-51\cdot3/(13\cdot2 - 5\cdot0 \times 13\cdot1)$

and

$(65\cdot0 \times 15\cdot73 + 71\cdot0 \times 13\cdot51 - 13\cdot0 \times 13\cdot53)/(3\cdot01 + 7\cdot01)$

2   Write a program to calculate the mean of the six items

$$15\cdot5, \quad 21\cdot3, \quad -7\cdot2, \quad 3\cdot5, \quad -1\cdot2, \quad 11\cdot1$$

Note: The mean is defined as the sum of all the items divided by the number of items. The Greek capital letter Σ (pronounced sigma) means 'the sum of', so if there are six items, $x_1, x_2, \ldots, x_6$, the algebraic expression for the sum of all the x's is

$$\sum_{i=1}^{6} x_i \text{ which is often shortened to } \Sigma\, x.$$

2.7 Programming forms

Before any information can be read into a computer, it has to be prepared either as a pack of cards punched with holes, or as a roll of paper tape punched with holes. This work of transcribing from the hand-written program to the cards or paper tape is called 'punching'. It is rather similar to typing and it is carried out on special card or tape punching machines, usually by typists specially trained to do this work. It is most important therefore that the work you prepare for this punching process is very carefully and legibly written. To help you to do this, special programming forms are often provided. These are printed with squares, eighty squares to a line. Only one symbol is written in one square.

If you have no special programming forms, ordinary paper, printed with $\frac{1}{4}''$ squares, can be used instead. In this case, draw a vertical line after the 6th column, and another one after the 72nd column. When we are writing out a program, the first six columns are used for special purposes, which will be explained later. The columns after the 72nd column are not used in normal programs, although every punched card has in fact eighty columns on it.

In order to make quite certain that the hand-written program is punched properly, special conventions are used. The letter O is often written Ō with a bar over it, to distinguish it from the digit 0 (nought), which is written Ø with a stroke through it. The letter I should be written with the cross bars at the top and bottom to distinguish it from the digit 1 (one), and the letter Z should be written Ƶ with a bar through it to distinguish it from the digit 2 (two). These are the letters and digits which most often get confused.

Only one line of program must be written on one line, however short the line of program may be. Spaces can be put anywhere in order to make the line easier to read. It is usual to start every line at the seventh column, though any column after the seventh can be used if you prefer it.

Thus we can write a line of program as:

$$A=5 \cdot 6$$

or as	$A = 5 \cdot 6$
or as	$A \quad = \quad 5 \cdot 6$
or even as	$A = 5 \cdot 6$

Exercises 2.5

Write out the exercises you have done so far on proper program forms.

2.8 Integers

So far, we have not used the letters I, J, . . . , N to represent items in arithmetic expressions. These letters are used to denote integer quantities, that is positive or negative whole numbers, written without the decimal point. The letters A, B, . . ., H and Ō, P, . . ., Z always represent positive or negative decimal quantities. This distinction between integers and decimal numbers runs through all programming languages and must always be strictly observed.

We should always avoid defining a decimal quantity by an

B

integer expression. Thus it is better to write

$$A = 15 \cdot 0$$

rather than $\qquad$ $A = 15$

with no decimal point. Indeed some Fortran compilers will reject this second expression completely. Also we should try to avoid the definition of a decimal quantity by a mixed expression containing both decimal and integer quantities. For example, we should avoid such expressions as

$$B = C + I$$

since here B and C are decimal quantities and I is an integer quantity. Again it is better to write

$$C = B - 5 \cdot 0$$

rather than $\qquad$ $C = B - 5$

As a general rule, any expression defining a decimal quantity should be written entirely in terms of decimal constants and decimal variables.

Exercises 2.6

Rewrite the following expressions, so as to avoid mixing decimal and integer items.

1 $\quad$ $A = B - 7 + C$
2 $\quad$ $H = K + J - 8 \cdot 0$
3 $\quad$ $Q = X * 4$
4 $\quad$ $Z = -2B$
5 $\quad$ $W = N5 \cdot$
6 $\quad$ $P = \bar{O} * L * 5 \cdot 0$

Similarly, the items which are restricted to be integer quantities should not be equated to items which are written with a decimal point or to variables which represent decimal quantities. Thus it is right to write

$$I = J + 10$$

but we should not write

$$K = L + 3 \cdot 0$$

even though 3·0 is a whole number, since it has been written with a decimal point. Also it is wrong to write

$$M = N + P$$

since P represents a decimal variable, and M represents an integer.

Integer quantities can be used in expressions containing the arithmetic operators $+$, $-$, and $*$. Thus we can put

$$I = (J + K) * (L - M) * N$$

and the answer will always be an integer, since J, K, L, M and N are all integers, and the result of adding, subtracting or multiplying two integers will always be an integer. But we should take great care if we write

$$I = J/K$$

for although I, J and K are integers by definition, we cannot be certain if the result of dividing J by K will be an exact integer or not.

If it is not an exact integer, the compiler will ignore the decimal part of the answer and set I to the nearest integer whose absolute value does not exceed the true result. For example

$$I = 7/3$$

would set I to the value 2, and

$$J = -15/8$$

would set J to the value -1. Thus such constructions are best avoided as they can very easily lead to wrong answers.

Exercises 2.7

Say if the following programs are wrong, and write out correct versions. State what you think is the final value of K in each case.

1   I = 10
     J = 11
     K = (I + J)/7
2   I = 3
     J = 2
     K = 1/J

if it should be J instead of 1

result would be 1 ANS

3   I = 4
    J = 3
    K = (1 − I − J)/(I + J)

Answers: **1** K = 3   **2** K = 1   **3** 0

2.9 Exponentation

Exponentation is the act of raising a number to a given power. Thus the expression $2^3 = 8$ is the same as $2 \times 2 \times 2 = 8$. The small figure 3 is the power to which 2 has to be raised, that is the number of times 2 has to be multiplied by itself, in order to produce 8. The special symbol ** (double star) is used in Fortran to indicate the act of raising an item to any power. Thus we can write:

$$A = 3 \cdot 0$$
$$B = 2 \cdot 0$$
$$C = B ** A$$

and C will have the value 8·0. In its most general form the result

> C is always a decimal quantity, the item
> B is any decimal expression,
> and the power A is any decimal or integer expression.

In this example we have used a decimal quantity A as the power. We could have written instead:

$$I = 3$$
$$B = 2 \cdot 0$$
$$C = B ** I$$

since the expression for the power can be an integer expression or a decimal expression.

Examples 2.5

1   Calculate 5^{10}

$$A = 5 \cdot 0$$
$$I = 10$$
$$B = A ** I$$

2   Calculate $\sqrt{5}$. We could write

$$A = 5 \cdot 0$$
$$C = 0 \cdot 5$$
$$B = A ** C$$

or alternatively

$$A = 5 \cdot 0$$
$$B = A ** 0 \cdot 5$$

or even more simply, the single order

$$B = 5 \cdot 0 ** 0 \cdot 5$$

3 The logical statement

3.1 Labels

Normally, orders in a program are obeyed by the computer in the same sequence as they are written in the program, and the lines of the program can be thought of as being numbered 1, 2, 3 and so on. In the early days of programming, these numbers were entered in the first five columns of a line of program and the lines of program were identified by these numbers, which had to be kept in sequence. This was found rather inconvenient in practice, because every time an extra line was inserted into a program all the following lines had to be renumbered and any orders containing references to these renumbered lines had to be altered. For example, the simplest form of a jump order was

$$\text{GOTO } n$$

where n was the number of the line containing the next order to be obeyed in the program. We might have the lines:

$$
\begin{aligned}
1 \quad & A = 5 \cdot 0 \\
2 \quad & B = 3 \cdot 0 \\
3 \quad & C = A + B \\
\hline
14 \quad & \text{GOTO } 2
\end{aligned}
$$

in a program. If now we wanted to insert one line, say

$$D = 4 \cdot 0$$

we had to renumber everything thus:

$$
\begin{aligned}
1 \quad & A = 5 \cdot 0 \\
2 \quad & D = 4 \cdot 0 \\
3 \quad & B = 3 \cdot 0
\end{aligned}
$$

$$4 \quad C = A + B$$
$$5 \quad E = B + D$$
$$---------$$
$$16 \quad \text{GOTO 3} \qquad G\omega \; T\omega \; 3$$

and this would involve repunching all the program.

It took about five years from the start of electronic computing before the concept of a label occurred to programmers. The label is a positive integer which can be written anywhere within the first five columns of the program card. It is no longer the number of the line of program, but can be any integer between 1 and 9999. Thus the above example would be written:

$$A = 5{\cdot}0$$
$$2 \quad B = 3{\cdot}0$$
$$C = A + B$$
$$----------$$
$$\text{GOTO 2}$$

in the first place and corrected to:

$$A = 5{\cdot}0$$
$$D = 4{\cdot}0$$
$$2 \quad B = 3{\cdot}0$$
$$C = A + B$$
$$E = B + D$$
$$----------$$
$$\text{GOTO 2}$$

Here the correction is made simply by punching the two extra cards and inserting them in their correct places in the program pack. The number used for the label is not connected in any way with the position in the program of the order to which it is attached. It is only a label to identify that particular line of program uniquely. It is not even necessary that the labels be defined in ascending order in the program. Thus it is perfectly correct to write:

$$50 \quad A = 3{\cdot}0$$
$$21 \quad B = 2{\cdot}0$$
$$---------$$
$$33 \quad \text{GOTO 50}$$

We can define the labels in whatever order is most convenient to us as programmers.

3.2 The 'If' order

The conditional jump order or 'if' order in Fortran has the simple form

$$\text{IF (X)} \quad l, m, n$$

Here X represents any expression and l, m and n are integers defining three labels in the program. The labels do not need to be all different. Any two of the numbers l, m and n can be alike and refer to the same label.

The effect of the 'if' order is to interrupt the normal sequence in which the orders of the program are obeyed, by applying a numerical test to the current value of the expression X.

If $X < 0$ then the next order to be obeyed is that with the label l.

If $X = 0$, then the next order to be obeyed is that with the label m, and

If $X > 0$, then the next order to be obeyed is that with the label n.

Any one or two of the labels can refer to the next line in the program, that is to the order which would naturally be obeyed next if no test of the value of X took place.

The expression X within the round brackets can be any algebraic expression, in the general form of the 'if' order. It is very frequently just a simple integer, I, or a simple integer expression such as $I - 10$.

The effect of the 'if' order is always to cause the sequence in which the orders of a program are obeyed to change as the numerical value of the expression X changes.

For example:

```
          X = 3·0
    5     IF (X) 1, 2, 3
    1     A = 5·0
          STOP
    2     A = 6·0
          GOTO 4
```

3   A = 7·0
4   STOP

would set A equal to 7·0 since $X = 3·0 > 0$ when the test was obeyed. If however the order labelled 4 was altered to the pair of orders

4   X = X − 3·0
    GOTO 5

then the value of X would be zero when the test was obeyed a second time, and so A would equal 6·0 at that point. Then control would carry on over a third cycle so that $X = −3·0$ and $A = 5·0$ when the program finally reached the stop order.

3.3 The simple loop

One of the most important uses of the 'if' order is in the type of calculation which performs a simple action many times over. Suppose we want to repeat an action 100 times, for example suppose that we cannot sleep and we start counting mental sheep. Without any computer, we would simply keep a tally in our minds of the number of sheep. The tally starts at one and each time a sheep passes through our imaginary gateway, we advance the tally by one, one sheep, two sheep, and so on.

In the computer, we will call the tally by the name N, and the first step is to set N to the first value it must assume, that is

[Set N = 1]

Then we carry on with the necessary orders in the program to carry out the actions we want repeated 100 times, say

[Let one sheep pass the gate]

Then we add one to our tally, that is [Add 1 to N]
Next we test if N = 100,

⟨Does N = 100?⟩

If N is still less than 100, we go back to the orders which let one sheep pass the gate, since we have not let 100 sheep through. But if N does equal 100, we stop.

The flow chart for this simple loop would look something like this:

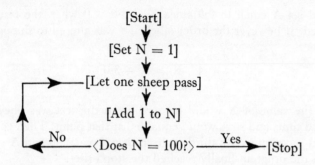

The relevant parts of the program would look something like this:

$$N = 1$$

99 $\left.\begin{array}{c} ----\\ ----\\ ---- \end{array}\right\}$ (orders which let one sheep pass)

$$N = N + 1$$
$$IF\ (N - 100)\ 99, 98, 98$$
98 STOP

Since the test in the 'if' order is

$$\langle Is\ X <, = or > 0? \rangle$$

and we want to test when $N = 100$ we have to set the quantity within round brackets to $N - 100$ and test when $N - 100 <$, $= or > 0$ so that if $N - 100 < 0$, that is if $N < 100$, control jumps back to the order with the label 99. But when finally $N = 100$, control goes on to the order with the label 98. Of course N never gets greater than 100, but we have to fill up the third label in the test, so we put 98 there as well.

Example 3.1

To form the sum $1 + \frac{1}{2} + \frac{1}{3} + \frac{1}{4} + \frac{1}{5} + \frac{1}{6}$ in A.

The flow chart should be drawn out first.

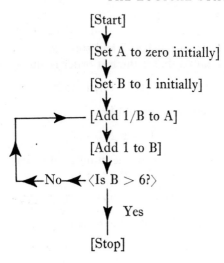

[Start]

[Set A to zero initially]

[Set B to 1 initially]

[Add 1/B to A]

[Add 1 to B]

No ← ⟨Is B > 6?⟩

Yes

[Stop]

The program follows from this quite easily, and is in fact much shorter than the flow chart, thus:

$$A = 0{\cdot}0$$
$$B = 1{\cdot}0$$
$$1 \quad A = A + (1{\cdot}0/B)$$
$$B = B + 1{\cdot}0$$
$$\text{IF } (B - 6{\cdot}0)\ 1,\ 1,\ 2$$
$$2 \quad \text{STOP}$$

Here is a table of the values of A and B at various points in the running of the program.

Initially $A = 0$ and $B = 1{\cdot}0$.

At the first test, $A = 0 + \frac{1}{1} = 1{\cdot}0$ and $B = 1 + 1 = 2{\cdot}0$, so $B - 6 < 0$ and we jump back to label 1.

At the second test, $A = 1 + \frac{1}{2}$ and $B = 2 + 1 = 3{\cdot}0$. $B - 6$ is still < 0, so we jump back to 1 again.

At the third test, $A = (1 + \frac{1}{2}) + \frac{1}{3}$ and $B = 3 + 1 = 4{\cdot}0$ and we jump to 1.

At the fourth test, $A = (1 + \frac{1}{2} + \frac{1}{3}) + \frac{1}{4}$ and $B = 4 + 1 = 5{\cdot}0$, so we jump back to 1 again.

At the fifth test, $A = (1 + \frac{1}{2} + \frac{1}{3} + \frac{1}{4}) + \frac{1}{5}$ and $B = 5 + 1 = 6{\cdot}0$, so $B - 6 = 0$ and we jump back to 1 for the last time.

At the sixth test, $A = (1 + \frac{1}{2} + \frac{1}{3} + \frac{1}{4} + \frac{1}{5}) + \frac{1}{6}$, which is the desired value and $B = 6 + 1 = 7 \cdot 0$, so that $B - 6 > 0$ and we carry on to the order labelled 2 and stop.

It should be noted that if the test order is altered say to

$$\text{IF } (B - 4 \cdot 0) \; 1, \; 1, \; 2$$

then the final value of A would be

$$1 + \tfrac{1}{2} + \tfrac{1}{3} + \tfrac{1}{4}$$

and similarly no extension to the number of orders in the written program is needed if we alter the test to

$$\text{IF } (B - 100 \cdot 0) \; 1, \; 1, \; 2$$

though in this case the final value of A is

$$1 + \tfrac{1}{2} + \tfrac{1}{3} + - - - + \tfrac{1}{99} + \tfrac{1}{100}.$$

It is usual for the count B to be set equal to 1 and the sum A to be set to zero before we enter the actual loop over which the count is to be carried out. This is to ensure that no spurious values are given to B or A, by accident. This process of setting the counts equal to unity and the summations equal to zero before the start of the main calculations, is called 'initialization of the variables', or more simply, 'clearing the store'. In this example the store named A and the store named B are the only two locations used to hold numerical information during the course of the calculation. Hence they are the only two storage locations which need to be initialized, that is set to the values we want them to assume at the start of the calculations.

Suppose for example that in the above program we had started off with the initial orders

$$A = 2 \cdot 0$$
$$B = 3 \cdot 0$$

and carried on as before with the orders

```
1   A = A + (1·0/B)
    B = B + 1·0
    IF (B − 6·0) 1, 1, 2
2   STOP
```

The program would have calculated

$$A = 2 \cdot 0 + 1 \cdot 0/3$$

and $\qquad B = 3 + 1 = 4 \cdot 0$

Then $\qquad A = 2 \cdot 0 + (1 \cdot 0/3) + 1 \cdot 0/4$

and $\qquad B = 4 + 1 = 5 \cdot 0$

$$A = 2 \cdot 0 + (1 \cdot 0/3) + (1 \cdot 0/4) + 1 \cdot 0/5$$

and $\qquad B = 5 + 1 = 6 \cdot 0$

and finally

$$A = 2 + \tfrac{1}{3} + \tfrac{1}{4} + \tfrac{1}{5} + \tfrac{1}{6}$$

and $\qquad B = 7 \cdot 0 > 6 \cdot 0$

Thus if we set wrong initial values, we shall get wrong results.

Similarly, we must be very careful to specify our jumps in the 'if' order exactly. Suppose in the above program the 'if' order had been written as

$$\text{IF } (B - 6 \cdot 0)\ 1,\ 2,\ 2$$

At the fifth test,

$$A = 1 + \tfrac{1}{2} + \tfrac{1}{3} + \tfrac{1}{4} + \tfrac{1}{5}$$

and $\qquad B - 6 = 0$

so the jump to the order labelled 2 would take place and the quantity $\tfrac{1}{6}$ would never get added to the sum called A.

3.4 An example on a simple survey

Another use of the 'if' order is in the various statistical processes which involve testing the size of some quantity and counting the quantity under different headings according to its size. As an example, let us consider the ages of a number of children. If the child is under 5 years of age it is counted as a baby, if it is 5 or more, but under 12, it is counted as a child, and if the child is 12 years old or over it is counted as an adolescent. We can make a program to test the age of each child and keep count of the number of children in each of the three groups,

0 to 4 years old, 5 to 11 years old and 12 years old or older

The first stage is to think about the problem and to analyse how

best to carry out the calculations. Here we shall need three stores
to keep track of the three counts. Let the count of adolescents be
called A, the count of babies B, and the count of children C. We
have used names starting with the initial letters of the quantities
we are counting and this is a very useful trick to remind the programmer, not the computer, what his program is intended to do.
The first step is to set the counts A, B and C to zero.

Next we need a sequence of orders to read in the age, G of one
child and to test which group the child falls in.

Finally we need to add one into the right group.

The flow chart for this part of a program could be:

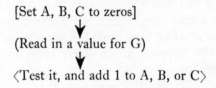

We shall see later how to construct a sequence of orders to read
one number, the age of a child, into the store called G. So now
let us consider the test section in detail. It could be something
like this:

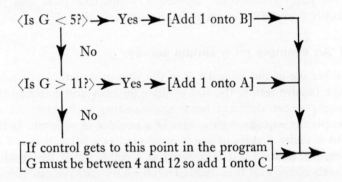

The next problem is that we wish to read in a whole sequence
of ages, and test them. So after the tests we must arrange simple
'Go to' orders to send control back to the 'Read in' section. Also
we must arrange a further test so that when all the data has been

read, control can go on to the next part of the program. Let us suppose that a child of negative age will signal the end of the sequence of data. With these refinements, the flow chart becomes:

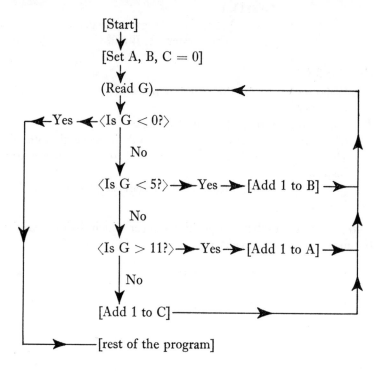

The sections of the program are:

$$A = 0\cdot0$$
$$B = 0\cdot0$$
$$C = 0\cdot0$$

```
1    - - - -⎫ orders to read one item of
     - - - -⎭ data into the store named G
     IF (G) 2, 3, 3
3    IF (G − 5·0) 4, 5, 5
4    B = B + 1·0
     GOTO 1
5    IF (G − 11·0) 6, 6, 7
```

7   A = A + 1·0
    GOTO 1
6   C = C + 1·0
    GOTO 1
2   - - - -⎱rest of the program, to print
    - - - -⎰the answers A, B and C

Exercises 3.1

1   Write programs for the exercises for which you have already
    drawn flow charts.
2   Draw flow charts and write programs:
    (*i*) to find the largest integer I which divides exactly into 26.
    Hint. Use repeated subtraction and test for a zero remainder
    instead.
    (*ii*) Using a similar trick, find the largest prime number I
    less than 30.

Note: A prime number is a positive integer which divides exactly
by no other integer except 1.

4 Input
and output

4.1 Read and write orders

Whilst the main body of the Fortran language does not vary from one computing system to another, the input and output orders are to some extent peculiar to each system itself. For this reason we describe first the simplest forms of these orders which will be interpreted correctly by the smallest compiling system as well as by the largest one.

The simplest input order has the form

$$\text{READ } (1,m) \text{ A}$$

where A is the name of the item to be set equal to the data to be read, and 1 is the number of the input to be used. Each input order refers to a special order called a format order, of the general form

$$m \quad \text{FORMAT } (\text{F5·2})$$

where m is a label, and the expression within the brackets is a sequence of symbols describing the pattern of the data to be read. In this case the F in F5·2 means decimal numbers, the 5 means that each of the numbers occupies in all not more than five columns, and the 2 means that two figures come after the decimal point. For example numbers like

$_\wedge 5\text{·}48, \; -3\text{·}49 \text{ and } _\wedge 9\text{·}57, \quad \text{where } _\wedge \text{ represents a space,}$

can all be read under this format. One column is allowed for the sign of the number and one column is allowed for the decimal point if it is present. The figures 5 and 2 can be adjusted in different format statements to match the pattern of the data. Thus, if each item in the data had not more than four figures in all, of which three figures come after the decimal point, the format would be F6·3 and numbers like

$$_\wedge 8{\cdot}975 \quad _\wedge 0{\cdot}621 \quad -1{\cdot}002 \quad -0{\cdot}007$$

could be read in. The F format can be used to read both positive and negative numbers, provided only that the decimal point is always in the same place in the pattern and that one column is allowed for the negative sign, or a space, if the number is positive.

Example 4.1

The format F12·5 will read in numbers like

$$_{\wedge\wedge\wedge\wedge} -0{\cdot}00001 \quad _\wedge 56789{\cdot}00000 \quad _{\wedge\wedge\wedge} -71{\cdot}08971$$

Exercises 4.1

Write out three format orders to be used in reading the following groups of numbers:

1	8171·00	−2·35	7·61
2	71·00	−25·51	6·07	−0·02
3	0·001	0·003	−0·001	1·000

The format order is an example of a special type of order called a non-executable order. It is needed in the program simply to hold information about the pattern the data is expected to have. When orders are being obeyed in their natural sequence, control can be thought of as 'skipping over' the format orders. Control can never pass to a format order. For this reason, we must never try to jump to a format order, by inadvertently referring to a label attached to format order, in any of our jump orders.

When the program is compiled, the read order and the information in the format order are joined together by the compiling system to form one composite order,

READ (1,19) A
19   FORMAT (F5·2)

'read one item of data on input device 1, in the pattern defined at label 19, that is in the format, F5·2, and set the contents of the store named A equal to the input item'.

If the input data is not in the pattern defined by F5·2, the computer reports an error in the data which it is trying to read. For example, the read order

READ (1,19) I

would be treated as faulty when coupled with the format statement

19   FORMAT (F5·2)

as this read order is asking the computer to read in a decimal quantity in the pattern F5·2 and set an integer variable I equal to it, and integer variables should not be set equal to decimal quantities.

The columns on the card (or rows of paper tape) allowed to one item are called the field for that item. The first number in the F format is the maximum size of the field. If the item to be read has fewer digits than the F format specifies, the item will still be read correctly, provided only that the field for it is filled out to the correct number of columns by blank columns on cards or by space symbols on paper tape.

It is necessary when using punched cards for the input of data to specify the field for each item accurately, but the compiler, when asked to interpret the format orders for input, usually has built into it an 'over-rider' so that, provided the number on the card or tape is punched with a decimal point, it will be read correctly by the program, even though the format specifies a position for the decimal point different from the one it actually occupies.

The maximum number of digits that can normally be read into one storage location is 10, so that the largest field width that can be specified for decimal input or output is 12.

The corresponding form of output order is

WRITE (2,m) A

Here 2 is the number of the output device, usually a lineprinter, the answer to be printed is the current numerical value of A and m is the label attached to a format order,

m   FORMAT (F5·2)

where F5·2 defines the pattern in which the result is to be printed. Before each item is printed there is output either, one space if the number is positive or, a minus sign if the number is negative. The decimal point is printed in the position defined by the format statement, in this case in the third column of the field. Both the sign digit and the decimal point must be counted in calculating the total width to allow for the number, for example $-3{\cdot}67$ has a field five items wide, so has the number $_\wedge 7{\cdot}31$ with a space printed instead of a plus sign.

Let us consider again the example 2.1.4. We can now redesign it. Before, the four quantities which were to be added together were set explicitly within the program as equal to A, B, C and D respectively. If we had wanted to form the sum of four different items we would have had to rewrite the first part of the program. Now we assume that the four items are punched on four cards as data to be input and we can write one program to input any four items in the correct pattern, form their sum and print the result.

The program might be now:

```
4    FORMAT (F5·2)
     READ (1,4) A
     READ (1,4) B
     READ (1,4) C
     READ (1,4) D
     E = A + B + C + D
     WRITE (2,4) E
     STOP
```

From this example, we see that the same format order can be referred to by any number of read and write orders, provided only that the same data pattern is required by each read or write order.

We are now in a position to finish off the program for the example 3·4, by adding the read orders, at label 1, and the write orders at label 2:

```
1    READ (1,8) G
8    FORMAT (F6·1)
```

and

```
2    WRITE (2,8) A
     WRITE (2,8) B
```

WRITE (2,8) C
STOP

The read section will read in a pack of cards punched with the height of one child in inches on each card, in a layout with four figures before the decimal point and one figure after it.

The write section will print the three values A, B and C in the same pattern, one number on each line.

Exercises 4.2

Draw the flow chart and write programs to carry out the following calculations:

1   Read in two positive numbers, divide the first number by the second number and print the answer. Continue to do this until a negative number is read. Then stop the calculation.
2   Read in groups of four positive numbers. Form the sum of each group of four, divide each number by this sum and print the results. Again arrange that the program stops when a negative number is read.
3   Read in groups of seven positive numbers and print the percentage each is of the sum of each group, that is print $100x/\sum x$. Stop when a negative number is read.

Assume a format of three figures before the decimal point and one figure after the decimal point in all the above examples.

4   Consider what changes are needed in each program to alter the input pattern to two figures before the decimal point and two figures after it.

4.2 Simple lists

Suppose again that we have four numbers to input, all in the same pattern, as in the example of 4.1. There, we repeated the read order four times in the program in order to input the four numbers. Also we could only punch one number on each input data card and this left a lot of space on each card unused.

In order to avoid these difficulties, we introduce next slight extensions of the read and write orders and the format statements. These are:

$$\text{READ } (1,m) \text{ A, B, C, D}$$
$$m \quad \text{FORMAT } (4F5 \cdot 2)$$
$$\text{WRITE } (2,m) \text{ A, B, C, D}$$

Here the names of the locations concerned with the input (output) orders are stated in a list after the read (write) orders, and the number 4 of such items to be punched on one input card (or to be printed on one line of output) is stated before the pattern F5·2, in the format statement.

The list of items to be input (or output) as one unit is called one record. Thus, the end of a card usually marks one record in input from cards, and the end of one line usually marks the end of one record in input from paper tape, or in output to a lineprinter.

The number of items called for in a format statement must agree with the number of items stated in the read/write lists. Thus, if the card to be input contained the three numbers

$$_\wedge 3 \cdot 21 \quad -5 \cdot 63 \quad _\wedge 2 \cdot 53$$

the format order was

$$10 \quad \text{FORMAT } (4F5 \cdot 2)$$

specifying four numbers, and the read order was

$$\text{READ } (1,10) \text{ A, B, C}$$

ordering that three numbers be read, there would be no harm done, but if the record was

$$_\wedge 0 \cdot 24 \quad _\wedge 3 \cdot 21 \quad -5 \cdot 63 \quad _\wedge 2 \cdot 53 \quad -9 \cdot 12$$

with five items on the card and the same read and format orders, the fifth item, $-9 \cdot 12$, would be ignored completely.

Example 4.2

Suppose that we have a record punched

$$_{\wedge\wedge} -5 \cdot 39 \quad _{\wedge\wedge} 15 \cdot 20 \quad _\wedge 199 \cdot 32 \quad -200 \cdot 15$$

What read and format orders should we have? Firstly there must be four items in the input list, since there are four numbers in the record. Secondly these must be decimal numbers with not more than five figures in all, of which two come after the decimal point. Then the orders should be something like these:

99   FORMAT (4F7·2)
     READ (1,99) A, B, C, D

Here we have allowed one column for the decimal point, since it is actually punched, and one column for the minus sign, if the number is negative, or a blank if the number is positive. Thus there are seven columns allowed for each number.

4.3 Integer formats

Up to now we have only considered the input and output of decimal quantities to or from stores which can hold decimal numbers, with names A, B, – – –, H or $\bar{O}$, P, – – –, Z. It is also possible to input and output integer quantities, that is whole positive or negative integer numbers, to or from stores which can hold only integers and have names I, J, – – –, N. The pattern of the format is

$$I n$$

where n is the maximum number of digits expected in any one integer. Thus the pair of orders

9   FORMAT (I3)
    READ (1,9) M

would read into the store named M, a positive integer of up to three digits, or a negative integer with a — sign and one or two digits.

The extension to lists is obvious. The orders

7   FORMAT (3I2)
    WRITE (2,7) I, J, K

would print the three numbers in the stores named I, J, K on one line as integers with up to two digits each.

The maximum number of digits that an integer can have is usually seven so that, with the sign, the maximum width for an input/output field for integers does not need to be more than eight items.

As an example, suppose that these five integers

$$_{\wedge\wedge\wedge}9 \quad _{\wedge\wedge}55 \quad _{\wedge}101 \quad -221 \quad _{\wedge\wedge}-2$$

are punched on a card in five equal fields, each four columns wide. The input orders could be:

    6   FORMAT (5I4)
         READ (1,6) I, J, K, L, M

If we wanted to print them with at least one space between each number, the output orders could be

    7   FORMAT (5I5)
         WRITE (2,7) I, J, K, L, M

and this would avoid having no space between the numbers 101 and −221.

We can have specifications for both integer and decimal items in the same format statement.

Example 4.3

For a record punched with some integer items and some decimal items, thus:

$$_{\wedge}9 \quad 55 \quad _{\wedge}1\cdot35 \quad -0\cdot01 \quad 720$$

we could have the input orders:

    98   FORMAT (2I2, 2F5·2, I3)
         READ (1,98) I, J, A, B, M

Here the format statement has been extended to include several different patterns. The list in the read order must agree exactly, both in the number and the type of item, with the list of patterns in the format statement. We can make up a list of both integer and decimal numbers in any order, provided only that the list of patterns in the format statement agrees with the list in the read or write order.

4.4 Heading and terminating sequences

There are special cards placed at the head and tail of a pack of program cards which do not form part of the program itself. They are sometimes called control cards, since they control the input of the actual program cards.

Like input and output orders, these head and tail cards differ slightly between one computing system and another. We shall describe here the simplest form of heading cards to be used with an ICL 1900 system.

First there should be four blank cards in the pack. The first heading card is

PROGRAM (NAME)

punched in column 7 onwards. NAME represents the name you have given to your program and it must consist of four capital letters only. The next two cards describe the channels for input and output. They are fairly standard. The input card reader is represented by the number 1, and the output lineprinter is referred to by the number 2.

INPUT 1 = CR0
OUTPUT 2 = LP0

that is, input is to be on channel 1, card reader number 0 and the output is to be on channel 2, lineprinter number 0. The heading section is terminated by one card punched with the word

END

in columns 7, 8 and 9, and followed by one blank card. The next card is the heading card for the program itself. This is punched, starting in column 7,

MASTER NAME

Here NAME can have up to six characters, which can be letters or digits. The first character must be a letter, and it should be noted that here, unlike the program card, the name is not in round brackets. In short programs, the names on the program card and on the master card are usually the same.

This master heading card is followed by the main body of the program itself.

The last two cards of the program pack are another END card, followed by a card punched with the word

FINISH

in columns 7 to 12. The compiling process is terminated by these two cards. The 'finish' card has the effect of directing control from the end of the compiling program to the first order of your program.

There should now be four blank cards and then the first card of your input data, if any. After the pack of cards for the data to be input there should be four more blank cards. The whole pack should be checked very carefully to see that every card is in its correct place, before it is sent to the computer to be tested.

It is customary to use different colours of cards for the heading cards, the pack of program cards, the pack of data cards and the tailing cards.

For paper tape input, the conventions are very similar. First there should be at least six inches of run out tape, followed by a new line symbol, six spaces

    and the words PROGRAM (NAME), new line symbol
    six spaces INPUT 1 = CR0, new line
    six spaces OUTPUT 2 = LP0, new line
    six spaces END, new line

about one inch of run out tape, new line

    six spaces MASTER NAME, new line

the sequence of orders in the program itself and finishing with a new line,

    six spaces END, new line
    six spaces FINISH, new line

about four inches of run out, new line

    the data to be input, finishing with new line,

about four inches of run out, new line

    'end of tape' symbol, and at least six more inches of run out.

Example 4.4

The complete pack of heading cards, program cards and data cards for our example to form the sum of four numbers might be:

> five blank cards
> PROGRAM (TEST)
> INPUT 1 = CR0
> OUTPUT 2 = LP0
> END
>
> one blank card
> MASTER TEST
> 4   FORMAT (F5·2)
> READ (1,4) A
> READ (1,4) B
> READ (1,4) C
> READ (1,4) D
> E = A + B + C + D
> WRITE (2,4) E
> STOP
> END
> FINISH
>
> four blank cards
> ∧ 3·75
> ∧ 2·11
> ∧ 1·93
> ∧ 1·38
> four blank cards

For IBM computers, the usual conventions for headings are that all control cards start at column 1 with a solidus sign, /.

A typical heading might be:

four blank cards

// SMITH JOB	This is to tell the computer it has a job to do for the user named SMITH. The name is punched in columns 3–12 and JOB in columns 13–15.

// PROG 1 EXEC FORTRAN

This is to tell it to translate the program called PROG 1. PROG 1 is punched in columns 3–12 of the card. The word EXEC is in columns 13–16 and FORTRAN is in columns 20–26. This tells the computer the translation is from Fortran to basic machine code.

program cards in Fortran

The cards for translation are finished by one card

END
/*

with END punched in columns 7–9 and one card with /* in columns 1 and 2.

// EXEC PROG 1

The name PROG 1 is punched in columns 11 onwards. This card tells the computer to start obeying the orders in the program called PROG 1 starting with the first executable order in the program.

data cards
/*

The pack of data cards finishes with one card punched /* and the whole pack finishes with an END OF JOB card.

// END OF JOB

This card terminates the run.

The whole pack of cards must end with at least four more blank cards.

4.5 How to get your program running

We now have all the concepts needed to write many programs. These concepts have all been expressed in their very simplest forms, so that the student can get on to the actual writing and testing of programs on a computer as quickly as possible. Like most other human activities, in programming, practice makes perfect. The later chapters in this work will be concerned with more sophisticated expansions of the ideas we have used already, but we are now in a position to get a lot of practice in writing real programs. The student should make sure at this point that he has fully understood the three basic types of orders, the simple forms of program heading described above and the concept of the flow chart before he goes on to study the more complicated concepts to be described later.

The method to be followed for each programming example should be something like this:

1   Decide how you are going to carry out the calculations. In small calculations this is often the same as writing out the steps you have to go through to carry out the calculation with the aid of a desk calculator.

2   Work out by hand the answers expected from a small set of sample data and make sure that the method you propose for carrying out the calculations really works.

3   Check for any special problems and devise tests to guard against them, such as tests for not trying to divide by zero, or for not trying to form a negative square root. Revise your proposed method of doing the calculations as needed until you think it is foolproof.

4   Decide exactly what answers must be printed and the patterns you want them to be printed in.

5   Draw up a flow chart, showing all possible paths for control to take in your program.

6   Write out the actual orders required in the program, remembering to write out the correct heading and terminating sequences in each case. Include in your program the extra orders for printing the intermediate results at each stage of your program as an aid to checking your calculations.

7   Write out your set of test data in the pattern required by the program, ready to be prepared as input to the computer.

8   In the bigger computing installations, the actual punching of

the paper tape or punched cards will be done for you. In the smaller laboratories you will have to do this for yourself. So the next step is to punch or get punched your heading, program and data. Check very carefully indeed at this point that the punching has been done correctly and the input has been prepared properly.

There are several faults which may stop an input reader from reading a paper tape properly. You should check for any slight tears in the tape, particularly around the sprocket holes, or any variation in the thickness or opacity of the paper tape. These faults can be seen by the human eye. More subtle faults are slight mis-spacing of the holes along the tape or slight variations in the size of the holes. These faults can only be checked by a special gauge which is usually supplied with the tape punching machine. Paper tapes intended for input to a computer must be labelled properly, wound up tightly and stored in cardboard boxes. They must not be folded or creased in any way.

Most of the points made above about punched paper tape apply to punched cards as well. All the holes in the cards must be punched cleanly and accurately and the cards must be stored in proper boxes. In particular the corners of the cards must not be bent.

For each run on the computer a ticket has to be filled in, giving to the operators such information as your name, the name of the compiler required, in your case Fortran, how long you expect the calculation to last, what sort of input and output you expect. It is most important that you fill in this ticket correctly and fully for each run on the computer.

Clear up any doubts you may have that the input has not been prepared properly.

9   Send your program and data with its ticket for a test run on the computer. No program ever works properly at the first, second or even at the third try so do not expect perfect results at this stage. You will almost certainly find that the compiler has discovered some faults in your program. It will print a list of these for you. Get these faults corrected and

send your program in again for another test. This time it may compile properly, but only output some wrong or incomplete results. Check your output as far as it has gone against your own hand-worked example. Correct the faults found by you or by the compiler, recheck everything and send your work again to the computer for a test run.

10 Finally the happy day will dawn when your results come back from the computer and are all correct. You have not finished yet however.

11 Remove the extra print orders which you put in to help you to check your program and test it again with your check data.

12 When you are perfectly satisfied that all your output is correct and in the proper layout, you can send the final version of your program to the computer with the data for which you actually want to know the answers. Once your program is working properly on your test data, it will work properly on every other set of data which conforms to the same input pattern.

Exercises 4.3

Draw up flow charts and write programs to carry out the following calculations

1   Read in a group of numbers, $x_1, x_2, \ldots, x_5,$

Form the mean, $\bar{X} = \sum_{i=1}^{i=5} x_i/5,$

and print the group of numbers with their means removed, that is print $x_1 - \bar{X}, x_2 - \bar{X}, \ldots, x_5 - \bar{X}.$

Note: For those who are not familiar with this notation using suffixes, x_1 is simply a symbol for the first number in the group, x_2 is the symbol for the second number in the group, and x_5 is the symbol for the fifth, that is the last number in the group when 5 is the number of items in the group.

2   Add to your program orders to form and print these other statistics, the sum of squares $\sum x_i^2$, and the sum squared $(\sum x_i)^2$ where in each case the summation is over five items.

3   Make a similar program to calculate and print the weighted mean

$$\bar{X} = (f_1 x_1 + f_2 x_2 + \ldots + f_5 x_5)/(f_1 + f_2 + \ldots + f_5)$$

where f_1 is the number of times the measurement x_1 occurs,

$$f_2 \text{ ,, ,,} \quad \text{,, ,, ,, ,,} \quad \text{,,} \quad x_2 \text{ ,,}$$

and so on.

4   The mean of the sum of the squared deviations of a set of data about its mean is called its variance. The formula is

$$v = \Sigma \{(x_i - \bar{X})^2/N\}$$

where the sum is over all the N items of data $x_1, x_2, \ldots, x_N$. Make a program to calculate and print the variance of a general set of data of N items.

2   Amend the above program to print the variances of several such sets of data, each with a different number of items.

4.6 The H format

Up to now we have met the F format for decimal items and the I format for integer items. There are many other types of format for special types of input and output.

One of the most useful of these is the H format, used on output only. So far, we have been able to output only decimal or integer numbers with no words to define what our answers represent. If there are more than a very few numbers in our results, we can very quickly get in a muddle as to what each number represents. The H format provides a way of giving a name to each item in our results.

For example,

        8   FORMAT (/18H SMITH'S ANSWER IS, F7·2)
            WRITE (2,8) A

would produce the line of output

        SMITH'S ANSWER IS −150·75

when the store A contains the quantity −150·75.

In the format statement, the symbol / produces a line feed

on the lineprinter and the number 18 before the H counts the number of symbols, including spaces which are to be output before the item A. All the symbols are counted from the first symbol after the H up to the comma before the F.

Example 4.5

Rewrite the end of the example 3.1, giving separate formats for the write statements, so that it will print titles for the answers.
   The two amended orders are

```
2   WRITE (2,10) A, B, C
10   FORMAT (/8 HADULTS =, F7·2, 7 HBABIES
     =, F7·2, 10 HCHILDREN =, F7·2)
```

This could produce the line of output

   ADULTS = 150·00 BABIES = 270·00 CHILDREN = 98·00

Exercises 4.4

1   Rewrite the programs you have already worked out, adjusting the output orders to print all the necessary names for the output results.
2   Draw a flow chart and write a program to print the mode of the following set of data:

   421, 480, 497, 487, 486, 421, 360

   Note: The mode is simply the largest item in the data.
3   Add orders to the above program to print the median of the data arranged in ascending order.
   Note: Since we have an odd number of items in the data, the median is half the sum of the two middle values.
4   Adjust the program of exercises 2 and 3, so that it reads in groups of positive numbers of different lengths and prints the mode and the median of each group.
   Note: For a group of data with an even number of items, the median is simply half the middle item.

c

4.7 The A Format

So far we have only input numerical data. Sometimes it is necessary to input or output alphabetic information as part of the data. This is done by the A format. For example the two orders

    36   FORMAT (8A1)
          READ (1,36) A, B, C, D, E, F, G, H

would read an input card

    PQRSTUVW

punched with the eight symbols in its first eight columns, and the computer would set

    the pattern for the letter P in the store called A,
    the pattern for the letter Q in the store called B,

and so on. The output from the order

    WRITE (2,36) A, B, C, D, E, F, G, H

with the same format order would produce the symbols

    PQRSTUVW

printed on one line as output.

More than one alphabetic item can be stored in one location. Thus

    36   FORMAT (2A4)
          READ (1,36) A, B

would read the record

    PQRSTUVW

and store the four letters PQRS in the store named A, and the four letters TUVW in the store named B. The order

    WRITE (2,36) A, B

with the same format order would then output one line of print

    PQRSTUVW

The maximum number of letters that can be stored in one location varies according to the design of the computer. It is usually eight for ICL computers and four for IBM computers. This difference gives trouble when a program, which runs well on an ICL computer, has to be transferred to an IBM one.

Sometimes, in input, we need to ignore some items in each record. This can be done by the X format. Thus the format orders

4   FORMAT (10X, 3 F7·2)
    READ (1, 4) A, B, C

would cause the first ten columns of each card to be ignored and the next 21 columns would be read as three decimal numbers occupying seven columns each. In output, 10X would cause ten spaces to be printed.

4.8 The continuation symbol

When we write format statements with long names to be output, like the one in the previous paragraph, we soon find that one card with 66 usable columns is not big enough to accommodate all the symbols in our expression. In such a case we can use a continuation symbol,

1

which must be punched in column 6 of the continuation card. This column, column 6, is called the continuation column. Then we can continue punching our order on several more cards, provided only that each continuation card has a 1 punched in the correct column, column 6, and the continuation of the order is punched in columns 7 to 72.

The same is true of paper tape input. Here the 1 has to be preceded by five spaces, from the preceding new line symbol.

Any card which has a letter C punched in its first column is ignored by the compiler. Thus comments or titles which are helpful to the programmer can be included on cards in the actual program pack, for example,

        MASTER TEST
    C   THIS IS MY FIRST TEST   A. BROWN
    9   FORMAT (5F7·2)

When we are using paper tape for the input of a program the same conventions apply, that is, any sector of tape which, when printed, starts with a C as its first symbol after the new line symbol, is ignored by the compiler, as far as the next new line symbol.

The line feed from one line of output to the next, on the line-printer, is usually controlled by the first symbol of the format statement which goes with the write order. A new line of printing is started each time a write order is obeyed. An extra line feed can be obtained by writing the format as

m   FORMAT (1H ,

with one space between the H symbol and the comma.

A '0', nought, in place of the space, thus

m   FORMAT (1H0,

would produce two line feeds, and a '1'

m   FORMAT (1H1,

would produce a feed of the paper onto the start of a new page.

These conventions usually imply that we have to have different format statements for read and write orders, even when they are for the same items of data. The read format needs no H symbols, while the write format usually has to have at least one H symbol to control the printing.

Exercise 4.5

Write down what you think would be the output from this program:

```
    MASTER
 C  OUTPUT TEST
 1  FORMAT (I3, 2X, I5)
-2  FORMAT (1H0, 5X, 5H A = ,I6, 5H B = ,I8)
 3  FORMAT (F5·2, F5·3, 5X, F5·0)
-4  FORMAT (1H0, //, 5X, 7H SUM = ,F7·2, 4X, 9H
 1     TOTAL = , F7·4 / 8H MEAN = ,F6·1)
 5  FORMAT (2A6)
-6  FORMAT (1H0, 6H NAME,,A6 / 9H ADDRESS,,A6)
```

```
READ (1, 1) I, J
READ (1, 3) A, B, C
READ (1, 5) Y, Z
WRITE (2, 2) I, J
WRITE (2, 4) A, B, C
WRITE (2, 6) Y, Z
STOP
END
```

with this as the input data:

$$100 \wedge\wedge -2917$$
$$2\cdot712\cdot350 \wedge 1 \wedge P \wedge| - \wedge 321$$
$$ANNIE \wedge 510A29$$

5 Loops and subscripted variables

5.1 Counting in a cycle

Suppose that, in our example above, § 4.1, we had wanted to form the sum of twenty numbers instead of only four. It would have been very wasteful of both programming effort and computer space, if we had to repeat the 'read' order twenty times in order to read in the twenty numbers. Instead we try to organize the program so that one cycle of orders is obeyed twenty times, instead of writing out twenty orders each of which is to be obeyed only once.

This is a very important part of programming technique. We must always try to write our programs to be as general as possible and to take as much advantage as we can of repetitive loops in the course of the calculation.

How can we do this in the present case? Let us set the quantity E, which will contain the final sum, to be equal to zero in the first place. Then we need to provide some mechanism in the program to repeat the 'Read A' order, and to add A to E twenty times exactly.

The mechanism to do this is a simple loop. We set an integer count, usually called I, to the value one initially, and then we add one onto the current value of I each time that we repeat the read and add cycle, until I = 20. The 'read' order will then have been repeated twenty times, and we can print our result, the final value of E.

The flow chart will look something like the diagram opposite.

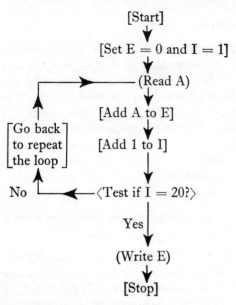

The heading cards are exactly the same as they were before, but now the program itself is something like this:

```
        MASTER TEST
4       FORMAT (F5·2)
        E = 0·0
        I = 1
1       READ (1,4) A
        E = E + A
        I = I + 1
        IF (I − 20) 1,1,2
3       FORMAT (/6H SUM =, F5·2)
2       WRITE (2,3) E
        STOP
        END
```

The data pack consists of twenty cards each punched with one number in the pattern F5·2, that is a signed decimal number with one figure before the decimal point and two figures after it.

5.2 Subscripted variables

Up to now, we have defined the use of only the 26 letters of the alphabet to represent decimal or integer quantities in our programs. But in longer calculations, we soon find that we need to define and to use many more variables than just these 26. There are several ways of providing these extra variables. The first, and most important, is to use subscripted variables. We have already seen how we can think of a sequence of storage locations as having the names A, B, – – –, Z. Now we can also define a sequence in the store as having the names

$$A(1), A(2), – – –, \text{up to say } A(100)$$

Similarly another sequence can be defined as having the names

$$B(1), B(2), – – –, \text{up to say } B(250)$$

Variables defined in this way are called subscripted variables.

Variables with names of this type occupy successive locations in the store, in sequence. Thus $A(2)$ follows $A(1)$ in the store and is followed by $A(3)$. The number in round brackets is called the subscript. The name of the whole sequence is the part of the name preceding the brackets, in this case the letter A. The subscript itself must be an integer such as 6, an integer variable such as I, or a simple integer expression, such as $I + 3$. The subscript must not be a decimal quantity since it always represents the position in the whole sequence A of the particular item $A(I)$.

Thus, in the sequence

$$X(1), X(2), – – –, X(10)$$

the sixth item will be referred to as $X(6)$ and the order

$$Y = X(6)$$

would set the variable named Y to the current value of the sixth item in the sequence called X. The order

$$Y = Z(1) + Z(5)$$

would set the variable named Y to the current value of the sum of the first and fifth items in the sequence named Z. The simplest form of a subscripted variable is

$$A(I)$$

where A can be replaced by any one of the letters A to H or Ō to Z, representing decimal quantities, and I can be replaced by any one of the integer letters I to N. The essential points to notice are that

A must be a letter representing a decimal quantity,
I must be either a letter representing an integer quantity, a simple
 integer number, or a simple integer expression,
 and the symbols for I must be enclosed in round brackets.

The resulting symbol A(I) can be used as the name of the decimal variable A(I) anywhere in algebraic statements, in exactly the same way as we used the simple letters A, B, – – –, H, or Ō, P, – – –, Z.

We must note, however, that if we use any letter A in this way to identify a sequence of subscripted variables, we cannot use the same letter A by itself in the same program as the name of a simple variable.

5.3 The 'dimension' statement

The computer automatically reserves storage spaces for the quantities represented by the letters A to Z. But the maximum length of each sequence of subscripted variables must be declared at the head of the program, so that the compiler can reserve storage space for these special sequences of variables, as well as for the ordinary variables used in the program. This reservation of space is done by means of a special heading card placed immediately after the MASTER card, and called the DIMENSION card. For example,

$$\text{DIMENSION A(100), B(250)}$$

would cause the compiler to reserve one sequence of 100 stores called A(1), A(2), – – –, A(100), and a second sequence of 250 stores called B(1), B(2), – – –, B(250).

There is no upper limit to the length that can be set for such a sequence, except the amount of store available in the computer. It is good programming practice to make such sequences as short as possible, particularly in time-shared systems, where an extravagant definition can waste space in the store and actually hold up the running of someone else's program.

Example 5.1

Suppose that we wish to find the largest number in a group of ten positive numbers.

The flow chart might be:

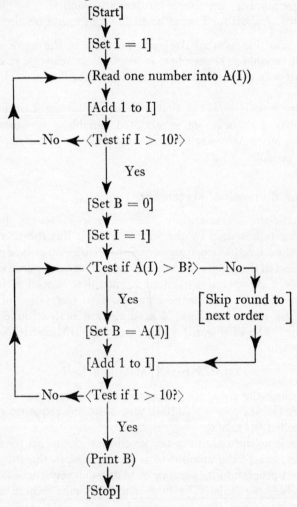

The heading cards might be:

```
PROGRAM (TEST)
INPUT 1 = CRØ
OUTPUT 2 = LPØ
END
```

The program cards might be:

```
      MASTER TEST
      DIMENSION A(10)
C     FIND LARGEST NUMBER IN THE GROUP
1     FORMAT (F6·2)
      I = 1
2     READ (1,1) A(I)
      I = I + 1
      IF (I − 10) 2,2,3
3     B = 0·0
      I = 1
6     IF (A(I) − B) 4,4,5
5     B = A(I)
4     I = I + 1
      IF (I − 10) 6,6,7
7     WRITE (2,8) B
8     FORMAT (/22H·THE·LARGEST·NUMBER·IS, F7·2)
      STOP
      END
      FINISH
```

The data cards might be:

```
512·31
210·52
500·76
927·70
252·52
291·76
815·23
275·96
927·11
200·09
```

The output should be

THE LARGEST NUMBER IS 927·70

Here the format for input is F6·2, that is a positive decimal number with three figures before the decimal point and two figures after the decimal point, which occupies 6 columns on a card.

5.4 'Do' loops

The above method of counting in a cycle is, strictly, all that we need in any program but an alternative method is provided in Fortran, particularly for use with subscripted variables. This method is based on the 'Do' order.

The simplest form of the 'Do' order is

$$\text{DO } m \text{ I} = 1, \text{ M}$$

where m is a label and M is an actual integer number, such as 6, or an integer variable, such as N.

The effect of this order is to repeat all the orders which follow the 'Do' order, up to and including the order labelled m. The first time these orders are obeyed I has the value 1, wherever it occurs in these orders. At each repeat, the value of I is advanced by 1 until, at the last repeat, I has the value M. Thus 1 is the value of I at the start of the loop and M is the value of I at the end of the loop. A few examples should make this clearer.

Example 5.2

Suppose we wish to form the sum, in B, of twenty numbers, named A(1), A(2), – – –, A(20). Previously we wrote:

$$\text{B} = 0{\cdot}0$$
$$\text{I} = 1$$
$$1 \quad \text{B} = \text{B} + \text{A(I)}$$
$$\text{I} = \text{I} + 1$$
$$\text{IF } (\text{I} - 20) \ 1,1,2$$
$$2 \quad \text{STOP}$$

As an alternative, producing exactly the same effect, but using the 'Do' order, we can write:

$$B = 0·0$$
$$DO \ 3 \ I = 1, \ 20$$
$$3 \quad B = B + A(I)$$
$$STOP$$

The mechanism of advancing the value of I by 1 and testing if I = 20 at each repeat, is carried out automatically, and the number of orders we have to write is halved.

Example 5.3

We can shorten the example about finding the largest of ten numbers very much, by using 'Do' loops thus:

```
    MASTER TEST
    DIMENSION A(10)
  C FIND THE LARGEST NUMBER IN THE GROUP
  1 FORMAT (10F 6·2)
    READ (1,1) (A(I), I = 1, 10)
    B = 0·0
    DO 4 I = 1,10
    IF (A(I) − B) 4,4,5
  5 B = A(I)
  4 CONTINUE
  2 FORMAT (/15H LARGEST NO. = , F6·2)
    WRITE (2,2) B
    STOP
    END
    FINISH
```

The data must now be punched with the ten numbers all on one card. The use of an implied 'Do' loop in the list for the read order should be noticed.

The order CONTINUE is introduced at label 4 to enable the jump over the order at label 5 to be interpreted without ambiguity by the compiler.

A vector is simply a sequence of numbers. Thus {1, 2, 3} is a vector, so is {4, 5, 6}. Two vectors with the same number of elements can be added together or subtracted one from the other.

Thus the sum of the two vectors above is the **vector**

$$\{5,\ 7,\ 9\}$$

and their difference is the vector

$$\{-3,\ -3,\ -3\}$$

Example 5.4

Suppose we want to write a program to read in a vector of ten items and to print the sum of all the items in the vector. First we need to prepare to form the sum in Z, by setting Z to the initial value zero. Next we have to read in the ten items punched as one number on one card or printed line of paper tape. We shall use a 'Do' loop to count over the ten items. Finally we have to print our answer.

The flow chart could be:

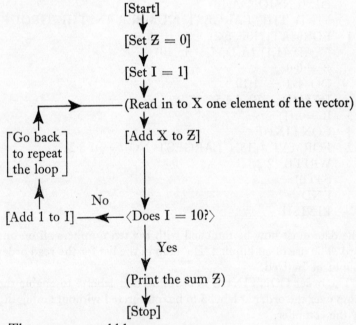

The program could be:

MASTER ADDVEC

1   FORMAT (F5·2)

```
    2   FORMAT (7H SUM = ,F6·2)
        Z = 0·0
        DO 3 I = 1,10
        READ (1,1) X
    3   Z = Z + X
        WRITE (2,2) Z
        STOP
        END
```

Exercises 5.1

1   Write a simple program to read in two vectors of five items each and print their sum.
2   Add orders to your program to print their difference as well.
3   Read in two vectors of 8 items each and print the sum of all their elements.
4   Add to your program, to print the two new vectors formed by dividing each element by the sum of all the elements.

The usual mathematical notation for a vector with n items is

$$\{a_1, a_2, - - -, a_n\}$$

and any element can be referred to as a_i, with a single suffix.

The similarity can be seen between this notation and the notation A(I) for the sequence A, explained above. If we want to read in such a vector, we usually read the number of elements N separately from the first data card, and then input the N separate elements of the vector $\{a_1, a_2, - - -, a_n\}$ into the sequence A(1), A(2), - - -, A(N).

We must first define the sequence A by a statement such as

DIMENSION A(100)

This sets 100 as the largest possible value of N and we can read into the A sequence a vector of any length up to 100 items. Our program should include a test of N to see that it does not exceed 100.

The start of such a program might be:

```
            MASTER READVEC
            DIMENSION A(100)
        1   FORMAT (I3)
            READ (1,1) N
```

IF (N − 100) 2,3,3
3   STOP
2   − − −

We can use any value of N greater than 100 to stop the program after we have read several such vectors.

Exercise 5.2

Adjust the program you wrote for exercises 3 and 4 above, to deal with vectors of any length.

A matrix is a two-dimensional array of numbers, e.g.

$$\begin{bmatrix} 0.1 & 0.2 & 0.3 \\ 1.1 & 2.3 & 4.5 \end{bmatrix}$$

Two matrices of the same size and shape can be added together simply by adding together corresponding elements, e.g.,

$$\text{let } A = \begin{bmatrix} 1.1 & 2.1 & 3.2 \\ 4.3 & 5.2 & 6.1 \end{bmatrix}$$

$$\text{and } B = \begin{bmatrix} 0.7 & 0.8 & 0.1 \\ 1.2 & 3.1 & 0.9 \end{bmatrix}$$

Then if $C = A + B$

$$C = \begin{bmatrix} 1.8 & 2.9 & 3.3 \\ 5.5 & 8.3 & 7.0 \end{bmatrix}$$

and if $D = A - B$

$$D = \begin{bmatrix} 0.4 & 1.3 & 3.1 \\ 3.1 & 2.1 & 5.2 \end{bmatrix}$$

Example 5.5

Suppose that we want to read in a matrix like A above, with two rows and three items in each row, and we want to print the sum of all six elements. First we have to set the sum Z to zero and then we have to count over all the elements. The flow chart would be something like the diagram opposite.

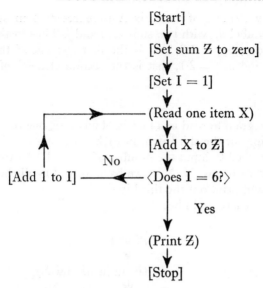

[Start]

[Set sum Z to zero]

[Set I = 1]

(Read one item X)

[Add X to Z]

No

[Add 1 to I] ────◀── ⟨Does I = 6?⟩

Yes

(Print Z)

[Stop]

The program might be:

```
    MASTER MATSUM
  1 FORMAT (F5·2)
  2 FORMAT (7H SUM = ,F7·2)
    Z = 0·0
    DO 3 I = 1,6
    READ (1,1) X
  3 Z = Z + X
    WRITE (2,2) Z
    STOP
    END
```

The similarity between this example, which reads a matrix as a single sequence of items, and the previous example, which reads a vector in the same way, should be noted.

Exercises 5.3

1   Write a program to read in two matrices A and B, and form and print their sum A + B.

2   Add to the program orders to print their difference A − B.

D

Any element of a matrix A is represented in algebra by the symbol $a_{i,j}$ with two suffices, i and j. Thus in the matrix A above, $a_{2,1} = 4\cdot3$, that is the first element of the second row, and $a_{1,2} = 2\cdot1$, that is the second element of the first row.

Example 5.6

Write a program to read in a matrix of any size, one row at a time and to print out the third item in each row.

First we need to input the number of rows M, and the number of items in each row, N. Next we have to read in all the items in each row and print out the third item.

The flow chart could be:

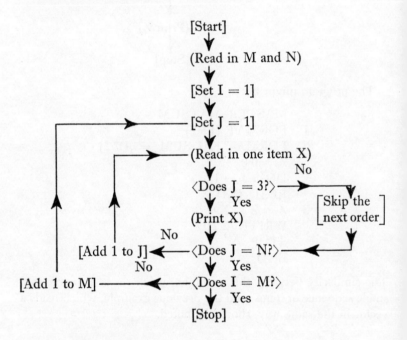

The program could be:

```
        MASTER INPMAT
    1   FORMAT (F5·2)
```

```
2  FORMAT (/18H THIRD ITEM OF ROW, I2,
 1      4H IS,,F5·2)
3  FORMAT (2I3)
   READ (1,3) M,N
   I = 1
6  DO 4 J = 1,N
   READ (1,1) X
   IF (J − 3) 4,5,4
5  WRITE (2,2) I, X
4  CONTINUE
   I = I + 1
   IF (I − M) 6,7,7
7  STOP
   END
```

Exercise 5.4

Read in a matrix of 6 rows, of 4 items each and print the sum of all the elements. Amend the program to read a matrix of any size.

5.5 Nested 'Do' loops

It is possible to nest one 'Do' loop inside another one. Suppose, for example, that we have as our data, a matrix with three numbers on each row and four rows, thus:

$$\begin{bmatrix} 1{\cdot}1 & 1{\cdot}5 & 1{\cdot}7 \\ 2{\cdot}2 & 2{\cdot}3 & 2{\cdot}5 \\ 1{\cdot}9 & 2{\cdot}1 & 2{\cdot}3 \\ 1{\cdot}7 & 2{\cdot}0 & 2{\cdot}1 \end{bmatrix}$$

and we want to form the sums of the items in each row, the sums of the items in each column and the sum of all the items. We let I be the counter of the rows and J the counter of the columns so that the suffixes i and j used in ordinary algebra are exactly similar to the counts I and J which we shall use in the double 'Do' loops. We design the program to be as general as possible so that it will read in a matrix with any number of rows and columns. The first thing we must do is to draw up our flow chart, thus:

[Start]

(1) ──▶── (Read m, the number of rows)

⟨Is $m \leqslant 0$?⟩ ➤ Yes ➤ [Stop]

   No

⟨Is $m > 10$?⟩ ➤ Yes ➤ (Write 'WRONG NO. OF ITEMS IN THE DATA')

   No

(Read n, the number of columns)

⟨Is $n > 10$?⟩ ➤ Yes ──────▶

   No

[Set $k = m \times n$ and $C = 0$]

(Read into the A sequence the $m \times n$ items of data which form the matrix)

[Clear the B sequence to hold the sums]

(Read the next item on the data tape)

⟨Is the item just read $-1\cdot0$?⟩ ➤ No ➤

   Yes

$$\left[\begin{array}{l}\text{For } i = 1 \text{ to } m \text{ and } j = 1 \text{ to } n, \\[2mm] \text{form} \quad b_i = \sum_{j=1}^{n} a_{ij}, \qquad b_{j+n} = \sum_{i=1}^{m} a_{ij} \\[2mm] \text{and} \quad c = \sum_{i=1}^{m}\sum_{j=1}^{n} a_{ij} \end{array}\right]$$

(Print b_i for $i = 1$ to m)

(Print b_j for $j = m + 1$ to $m + n$)

(Print c)

[Go back to (1)]

The layout of the data for each matrix is:

$$m$$
$$n$$
$$a_{11}\ a_{12}\ a_{13}\ \cdot\ \cdot\ \cdot$$
$$a_{21}\ a_{22}\ a_{23}\ \cdot\ \cdot\ \cdot$$
$$\cdot\ \cdot\ \cdot\ \cdot\ \cdot$$
$$a_{m,1}\ a_{m,2}\ a_{m\ 3}\ \cdot\ \cdot\ \cdot\ a_{m,n}$$
$$-1$$

The -1 at the end of each matrix is a check that we have got the correct number $m \times n$ of items in our data. Also the first number m on the data tape will act as a stop when this item is negative or zero.

Such checks are very important. It is very easy to leave out one item when punching a long sequence of numbers, or to punch one item twice over. Thus, a program for general use should always have as many checks like the one above as possible, in order that the correct number of items is input. The usual way to do this is to check that the item in the data stream immediately after the last item in the matrix has some special value, which does not occur in the main matrix. Thus, in a matrix in which all the elements are positive, we can check that this special item equals -1, or that it equals 9999, in a matrix in which no element is as great as 9999. We cannot make the computer check the actual digits punched, but we can make it check that the correct number of items has been punched and that each item is in the correct pattern, with the exact number of digits and the decimal point, if present, in its proper place.

The program might be:

```
   MASTER NEST
   DIMENSION A(100), B(20)
C  FORM ROW AND COLUMN SUMS OF MATRIX
1  FORMAT (I2)
8  FORMAT (100F5·2)
2  FORMAT ( / 9 H ROW SUMS, 10F5·1)
3  FORMAT ( / 9 H COL SUMS, 10F5·1)
4  FORMAT ( / 10 H TOTAL SUM, F5·1)
```

```
11    READ (1, 1) M
      IF (M − 10) 15, 15, 13
15    IF (M) 9, 9, 10
10    READ (1, 1) N
      IF (N − 10) 16, 16, 13
16    K = M * N
      READ (1, 8) (A(I), I = 1, K)
      K = M + N
      DO 5 I = 1,K
 5    B(I) = 0·0
      READ (1, 1) I
      C = 0·0
      IF (I + 1) 13, 12, 13
12    DO 6 I = 1, M
      K = N * I − N
      DO 6 J = 1, N
      B(I) = B(I) + A(K + J)
 6    B(J + M) = B(J + M) + A(K + J)
      DO 7 I = 1, M
 7    C = C + B(I)
      WRITE (2,2) (B(I), I = 1, M)
      WRITE (2,3) (B(I + M), I = 1,N)
      WRITE (2, 4) C
      GOTO 11
 9    STOP
14    FORMAT ( / 27 H WRONG NO. OF ITEMS IN
 1    DATA)
13    WRITE (2, 14)
      GOTO 9
      END
```

The lines

$$K = M * N, \quad K = M + N \quad \text{and} \quad K = N * I − N$$

are put into the program in order to simplify the structure of the loops, in the order

$$\text{READ (1, 8) (A(I), I = 1, K)}$$

in the loop   DO 5 I = 1, K

and in the inner loop:

$$\text{DO 6 J} = 1, \text{ N}$$
$$\text{B(I)} = \text{B(I)} + \text{A(K} + \text{J)}$$
$$6 \quad \text{B(J} + \text{M)} = \text{B(J} + \text{M)} + \text{A(K} + \text{J)}$$

Some of the smaller Fortran compilers do not allow multiplication within any of the integer expressions in 'Do' loops or in implied 'DO' loops such as occur in the read and write orders. In any case, it is good programming practice to calculate in the outer loop any complicated expression which involved only the subscripts which change in that outer loop. This is done in order to avoid repeated calculation of such expressions within the inner loops of a complicated program. Such repeated unnecessary calculating can slow down a program's running time on the computer, and make it use twice as much expensive machine time as a more efficient version, where the programmer has tried to avoid unnecessary repetition.

Thus in the above program if we had written the inner loop as:

$$\text{DO 6 J} = 1, \text{ N}$$
$$\text{B(I)} = \text{B(I)} + \text{A(N} * \text{I} + \text{J} - \text{N)}$$
$$6 \quad \text{B(J} + \text{M)} = \text{B(J} + \text{M)} + \text{A(N} * \text{I} + \text{J} - \text{N}$$

the multiplication of N by I would be carried out 2N times, each time the loop was obeyed, instead of only once by the order

$$\text{K} = \text{N} * \text{I} - \text{N}$$

outside the J loop.

The structure of the 'Do' loops in a nest should be need carefully, thus for three loops we might have:

$$\text{DO 1 I} = 1, \text{ M}$$
$$- - - - - - - -$$
$$\text{DO 2 J} = 1, \text{ N}$$
$$- - - - - - - -$$
$$\text{DO 3 K} = 1, \text{ L}$$
$$- - - - - - - -$$
$$3 \quad - - - -$$
$$2 \quad - - - -$$
$$1 \quad - - - -$$

and this would be correct. Either we must always finish the count implied by a loop properly, or we can leap out of an incomplete loop by means of an 'If' order, but we can never leap into a loop without having passed through the 'Do' order at an earlier point in our program in order to set the counts within the loop.

Thus:

```
          DO 1 I = 1, M
          DO 2 J = 1, N
          - - - -
   2      - - - -
   1      - - - -
```

is correct, so is

```
          DO 1 I = 1, M
          DO 1 J = 1, N
          - - - - -
   1      - - - - -
```

but

```
          DO 1 I = 1, M
          DO 2 J = 1, N
          - - - - -
   1      - - - - -
   2      - - - - -
```

is wrong since the J loop is not completed within the I loop. Similarly

```
          DO 1 I = 1, M
          - - - - -
          IF (X) 1, 1, 2
   1      - - - - -
          - - - - -
          - - - - -
   2      - - - - -
```

is correct since the 'Do' loop is either completed normally or the jump is made out of the loop to the line labelled 2. However,

```
        - - - - -
        - - - - -
        IF (X) 1, 1, 2
   1    - - - - -
        - - - - -
        DO 3 I = 1, M
        - - - - -
   2    - - - - -
        - - - - -
   3    - - - - -
```

is wrong, since it is possible for control to leap to the line labelled 2 within the loop, without having first passed through the order DO 3 I = 1, M. The rule is: never enter a loop except by passing through the 'Do' order.

Double loops can be used in the lists of read and write orders. For example, suppose that we want to print a number of arrays, each of a different size, that is we want to print M rows of N items in each row, and M and N may vary from one use of the program to the next one, so that we cannot define the size of the array we want to print in our dimension heading. The output orders might be:

```
   1    FORMAT (1H0/10F5·2)
        WRITE ((A(I,J),J = 1,N)I = 1,M)
```

These two orders would print a matrix of up to ten items on each row.

Exercises 5.5

Draw up flow charts and write programs to carry out the following calculations.

1 Read in a vector, containing both positive and negative items. Form the sum of the items, and print the new vector formed by replacing each positive item in the input vector by the percentage, that is by $100x/\sum x$, and by replacing each negative item by zero.

2 Read in a matrix of M rows of N items each, containing both positive and negative items, and print the matrix formed by

replacing each positive item by $100x/\Sigma\Sigma\, x$ (where $\Sigma\Sigma\, x$ is the sum of all the positive items in the matrix) and by replacing each negative item by zero.

5.6 Named variables

Another way of defining variables in a program is to give the variables names to remind us of what they represent in the calculation. For example suppose we wish to calculate interest at 5% per annum on a given capital sum of £5000 for two years, we might write the program:

$$A = 5000 \cdot 0$$
$$B = 5 \cdot 0 * A/100 \cdot 0$$
$$C = 2 \cdot 0 * B$$

using only our original decimal variables A, B and C, and the computer would perform the calculation quite correctly. However, another programmer, given this sequence of orders, would have no clue that A was a capital sum, B interest rate for one year and C the total interest. If, however, we can name the variables to remind us, as programmers, what the quantities represent, we might write the program as:

$$CAP = 5000 \cdot 0$$
$$RATE = 5 \cdot 0 * CAP/100 \cdot 0$$
$$TOTAL = 2 \cdot 0 * RATE$$

Some programmers find this naming of quantities very helpful, although the work of punching the cards is increased and the time taken to input the cards is also slightly increased. A name, when used in this way, must start with one of the letters A to H or Ō to Z if it represents a decimal quantity, or one of the letters I, J, K, L, M or N if it represents an integer quantity. A name should have not more than six letters or digits in it and it must always start with a letter and be followed by a symbol other than a letter, or a digit, or a space. Spaces are ignored by most compilers, so that the name ITEM 1 will usually be treated as the same name as ITEM1.

We can also define arrays of named variables. Thus, suppose

that the example 5.3 to find the largest of ten numbers was really
to find the heaviest of ten men, we might write it thus:

```
      MASTER TEST
      DIMENSION WEIGHT(10)
   1  FORMAT (10 F6·2)
      READ(1,1) (WEIGHT(I), I = 1,10)
      WMAX = 0·0
      DO 4 I = 1,10
      IF (WEIGHT(I) − WMAX) 4,4,5
   5  WMAX = WEIGHT(I)
   4  CONTINUE
   2  FORMAT( /15H MAX WEIGHT IS ,F6·2)
      WRITE(2,2) WMAX
      STOP
      END
```

5.7 Real and integer statements

There are several other types of statement which usually occur
at the head of a program, either before or after the dimension
statement, but always before the first actual orders of the program. Two of the most useful of these are statements of the form

$$\text{REAL} \qquad \text{L,M,N}$$

and $$\text{INTEGER } \text{W,X,Y,Z}$$

These statements cause the compiler to over-ride the normal
rules that variables with names starting with the letter A to H
and Ō to Z always represent decimal quantities, and variables
with names starting with the letters I to N always represent
integer quantities. Thus the first statement above makes the compiler regard the variables L, M and N as decimal quantities, and
the second statement makes the compiler regard the variables
named W, X, Y and Z as integer quantities. Each statement
remains in force throughout the particular program that follows
it up to the next END card.

5.8 Arrays

It is possible, in Fortran, to define not only a simple sequence in one dimension such as

$$\text{DIMENSION}\quad A(250)$$

but also a two-dimensional array or matrix. For example the statement

$$\text{DIMENSION}\quad A(10,\ 10)$$

would cause the computer to reserve $10 \times 10 = 100$ stores for the array named A and the orders

$$2\quad \text{FORMAT } (10 \text{ F8·3})$$
$$\text{READ } (1,\ 2)\ A$$

would then cause the computer to read in 100 items in the format labelled 2, that is 10 decimal items on each card and 8 columns to each item.

The first 10 items would automatically be read into the stores named

$$A(1,1),\ A(2,1),\ .\ .\ .,\ A(10,1)$$

respectively, the next ten items into

$$A(1,2),\ A(2,2),\ .\ .\ .,\ A(10,2)$$

and so on, until the last ten numbers would be read into the stores named

$$A(1,10),\ A(2,10),\ .\ .\ .,\ A(10,10)$$

respectively.

A three-dimensional array can be defined and used in a similar way, thus:

$$\text{DIMENSION}\quad X(5,10,5)$$

would define an X array of $5 \times 10 \times 5 = 250$ items.

Example 5.7

A simple program to read in a matrix of fixed size and to print its row and column sums, using the concept of arrays, might be:

```
     MASTER ARRAYTEST
     DIMENSION A(10, 10), B(10), C(10)
C    PRINT ROW AND COLUMN SUMS OF MATRIX
1    FORMAT (100 F5·2)
2    FORMAT (9H ROW SUMS, 10F5·1)
3    FORMAT (9H COL SUMS, 10F5·1)
     READ (1, 1) A
     B = 0·0
     C = 0·0
     DO 4 I = 1, 10
4    B(I) = B(I) + A(I, J)
     DO 5 J = 1, 10
5    C(J) =   C(J) + A(I, J)
     WRITE (2, 2) B
     WRITE (2, 3) C
     STOP
     END
```

Exercises 5.6

Rewrite the previous examples on matrices using the concept of two-dimensional arrays to shorten your programs.

A more general form of the 'Do' loop is provided in most of the larger computing systems. This is

$$\text{DO } m \ I = L, M, N$$

Here m is a label and L, M, N are integers or integer expressions. The effect is again, to cause all the orders which follow up to and including the order labelled m, to be repeated. The first time these orders are obeyed, I takes the value L, wherever it occurs in these orders. At each repeat, the value of I is advanced by N, until, at the last repeat, I has a value $\leqslant$ M. Thus L is the value of I at the start of the loop, M is the value of I at the end of the loop and N is the constant by which I is increased each time the loop is obeyed.

Example 5.8

Scan a set of data and form the sums of every third item and every seventh item. Suppose we have a program to read the N items of data into the A sequence, the rest of the program might be:

```
         B = 0·0
         C = 0·0
         DO 10 I = 3, N, 3
   10    B = B + A(I)
         DO 11 I = 7, N, 7
   11    C = C + A(I)
   12    FORMAT (2 F 10·3)
         WRITE (2, 12) B,C
         STOP
```

When it is considered that L, M and N can be quite complicated integer expressions and that such general loops can be nested up to three loops deep, even in quite small Fortran compilers, we can understand something of the complexity that can be built into a computer program. Some of the largest compilers will permit of nested loops up to 32 deep and subscripted variables defined in up to 16 dimensions.

Exercises 5.7

1   A class of twelve boys sits an examination consisting of three papers for each boy. Make a program to read in the name and the three marks for each boy. Print the actual sum of the marks for each boy and the percentage mark from 100. Also print the total marks given for each paper and express these as percentages of 100.
     Hint: Use alphabetic input for the names of the boys and store the names and the marks in a two-dimensional array. For example, the orders for input might be

```
   1    FORMAT (4A4,3F4·1)
        READ (1,1) ((A(I,J), I = 1,7) J = 1,12)
```

2   Add to your program orders to test which boy has the best marks and reprint the whole list of exam results in descending order of total marks, that is place the best boy first and the worst boy last on the list.

3   Rewrite your program making it more general, so that it will read in and check the names and marks of any number

M $\leqslant$ 100 of boys, each writing any number N $\leqslant$ 10, of exam papers, and print the exam results for one form of boys.

4 Add to your program to make it print all the exam results for the whole school.

6 Functions and subroutines

6.1 Built-in functions

The example on the calculation of the variance leads us naturally to ask the question 'Suppose we want to calculate the standard deviation (which is defined as the positive square root of the variance), how do we calculate the square root?' There are several ways to calculate a square root. For example, there is the recursive method, which goes back to Newton. Suppose we know that $x^2 = 50$. We make a guess, $x_0 = 7$, at the numerical value of the root, and then form $x_1 = \frac{1}{2}(x_0 + 50/x_0)$. This gives us a better approximation x_1, to the value of the root. We then form $x_2 = \frac{1}{2}(x_1 + 50/x_1)$ and repeat the process until the change at any cycle is very small. A program to do this might be, given the first approximation x_0 in X,

```
3    Y = 50·0/X
     Z = (X + Y) * 0·5
     IF (Z − X − 0·01) 2, 2, 1
1    X = Z
     GOTO 3
2    ------
```

But we have to form square roots every day and we do not want to have to repeat the writing out and punching of tape or cards for this section of program over and over again. So most compiling systems have a number of commonly used functions like $\sqrt{x}$ built into them automatically. In the case of Fortran compilers, we simply write the order

$$Y = SQRT(X)$$

and Y will be given the value of $\sqrt{X}$, where X is the value of the expression in round brackets at the time this order is obeyed.

Most compilers have built-in functions to perform the following calculations:

SQRT(X)   to give the positive square root of X
ALOG(X)   to give the log to base e of X
EXP(X)   to give e^x, the exponential of X
SIN(X)   to give the sine of X
COS(X)   to give the cosine of X

Also AINT(X) and X − AINT(X) give the integer part of X and

[Start]
↓
(1) ➤ (Read in N, the number of items)
↓
⟨Is N ⩽ 0⟩ —Yes→ [Stop]
↓ No
(Read the N items of data $x_1, x_2, --, x_N$)
↓
[Set the sum B, to zero initially]
↓
[Form $\bar{X} = \sum_{i=1}^{N} x_i$ in B]
↓
[Remove means, that is, form $x_i - \bar{X}/N$, for $i = 1, 2, --, N$]
↓
[Set a sum C to zero initially]
↓
[Form the sum of the squares, $\sum_{i=1}^{N} (x_i - \bar{X}/N)^2$ in C]
↓
[Form $D = +\sqrt{C}$]
↓
(Print the standard deviation, D)
↓
(1) ◄ [Go back to (1) to read more data]

the fractional part of X respectively, and I = IFIX(X) converts an expression from the decimal mode to the integer mode. Conversely X = FLOAT(I) converts an expression from the integer mode to the decimal mode, and ABS(X) gives the absolute value of X, that is the value of X with a positive sign. For example, if X = −5·3, the value of Y after the order Y = AINT(X) has been obeyed is Y = −5·0. Similarly if Z = X − AINT(X), Z = −0·3 and if I = IFIX(X), I = −5. When I = −5 A = FLOAT(I), so that A = −5·0, and finally B = ABS(A) gives B = 5·0.

Example 6.1

Let us now write a program to calculate the standard deviations of several sets (each of N items) of data x_1, x_2, − − −, x_N, where N can have a different value for each set of data. The flow chart might be as shown on p. 89.

The layout of the data is the value of N by itself on one card, the values of x_1, x_2, − − −, x_N, with up to 16 numbers on one card, each punched as a positive decimal number with two digits before the decimal point and two digits after it.

```
            MASTER STAD
            DIMENSION A(100)
    C       STANDARD DEVIATIONS
    1       FORMAT (100F5·2)
    7       FORMAT (I2)
    2       FORMAT (/6HS·D· =, F7·4)
    9       READ (1, 7) N
            IF (N) 8, 8, 6
    6       READ (1, 1) (A(I), I = 1, N)
            B = 0·0
            E = 0·0
            DO 3 I = 1, N
            E = E + 1·0
    3       B = B + A(I)
            DO 4 I = 1, N
    4       A(I) = A(I) − (B/E)
            C = 0·0
            DO 5 I = 1, N
```

```
5   C = C + A(I) * A(I)
    D = SQRT (C/E)
    WRITE (2,2) D
    GOTO 9
8   STOP
    END
```

Exercises 6.1

1 Write programs to form and print the following statistics from the same sets of data:
   (*i*) Three-year moving averages.
   (*ii*) Five-year moving averages.
   (*iii*) The data with the means removed.
   (*iv*) A three-year moving average of the data with means removed.
   (*v*) A five-year moving average of the data with means removed.
2 Add sections to these programs to form and print the standard deviations of the five sets of data you have produced.

6.2 General functions

If you require to use the same function several times over at different points in a program, and it is not a function which is built into the compiler, means are provided for you to program your own functions as you need them.

Suppose that we need to form x^5 in our program. We can define a decimal variable called XFIVE by the order XFIVE = X ** 5. Provided that the value of X has not changed meanwhile, every time later in the program that the quantity x^5 is wanted, we can write XFIVE, which has already the value of x^5, instead of re-calculating the expression X ** 5. This speeds up the actual process used by the computer and shortens the time taken to execute the calculation.

For example, to calculate

$$x^{15} + x^{10} + x^5$$

given the value of x in X, the program might be:

$$XFIVE = X ** 5$$
$$XTEN = XFIVE * XFIVE$$
$$XFIFT = XTEN * XFIVE$$
$$Y = XFIFT + XTEN + XFIVE$$

Up to now, our programs have only had one section called MASTER, apart from their heading cards and the data pack. Two other types of program sections are possible, called

FUNCTION NAME (X)

and   SUBROUTINE NAME (W, X, Y, Z)

sections. Just as the master program must have a name of four letters so must each function or subroutine have its own unique name. The packs of cards containing function or subroutine sections are usually placed after the heading cards, but before the Master program cards in the program pack, or on the program tape.

Each such section is terminated by the statements

RETURN
END

The whole program is terminated by the statement

FINISH

The simplest function has one parameter X. Each time the order,

$$Y = ANAME (X)$$

where ANAME is the name of the function, is encountered in the main program, the current value of X is used to form the quantity ANAME, the value of which is then given to the item called Y. The parameter X is sometimes called a dummy variable, since its actual value is not known until the order calling for the function is obeyed.

Example 6.2

Suppose we needed to form x^5 several times in one program. We have already seen one way of doing this, by defining a named variable. Alternatively we could have a section, defining a formal function, thus:

```
FUNCTION FIVE (X)
FIVE = X * X * X * X * X
RETURN
END
```

in our program pack, and in the master program we could then write orders of the form

$$A = FIVE (B)$$

as often as we needed them. Each time such an order was obeyed A would be given the current value of B^5 without any further programming on our part. Of course, expressions far more complicated than in this simple example can be treated as functions.

The name chosen for the function, in this example FIVE, must obey the usual rules for a name, that is it must start with one of the letters A, to H or Ō to Z if the quantity defined by the function is a decimal variable, or start with one of the letters I to N if the quantity defined by the function is an integer variable.

The simplest extension is to functions with more than one parameter. Thus, suppose that we want to form the positive root of a quadratic equation at several points in our program. The algebraic equation is

$$ax^2 + bx + c = 0$$

and the well-known formula for the positive root is

$$d = (b + \sqrt{(b^2 - 4ac)})/2a$$

We can define a function with three parameters A, B and C by the program section:

```
FUNCTION OSRT (A, B, C)
D = (B + SQRT (B * B − 4·0 * A * C))
OSRT = D/(2·0 * A)
RETURN
END
```

Here the root to be calculated is a decimal quantity, so the name chosen for the function, that is OSRT, must start with one of the letters A to H or Ō to Z.

Then in our main program, suppose we wanted the positive roots of the equations

$$2x^2 - x - 15 = 0$$

and

$$6x^2 + 11x - 10 = 0$$

we could put into our program the two orders

RT1 = OSRT (2·0, −1·0, −15·0)
RT2 = OSRT (6·0, 11·0, −10·0)

This first order would assign to the decimal variable RT1 the value of the positive root of the first equation, that is RT1 = 3·0, and the second order would assign to the decimal variable RT2 the value of the positive root of the second equation, that is RT2 = 0·66667.

It is important to notice that there is no connection between the names given to the parameters A, B, C in the section defining the function and the use of variables with the same names later on in other function sections, or in subroutines, or in the master part of the program. Thus we could write:

FUNCTION OSRT (A, B, C)
OSRT = (B + SQRT (B * B − 4·0 * A * C))/(2·0 * A)
RETURN
END
FUNCTION CUBRT (A)
CUBRT = EXP ((LOG(A))/3·0)
RETURN
END
MASTER TESTRT
A = OSRT (2·0, −1·0, 15·0)
B = CUBRT (0·5 * A)
– – – – – – –

After carrying out these first two orders in the master program, the variable A would have the value of the positive square root of the equation

$$2x^2 - x - 15 = 0$$

that is

$$A = 3·0$$

and B would have the value of $(\frac{1}{2}A)^{\frac{1}{3}} = (1·5)^{\frac{1}{3}}$.

This example should be studied carefully until the precise use of the dummy variables in the function headings is fully understood. The point is, that in the function sections of any program, the parameters of the functions have no precise numerical meaning at the time they are written in the function. They are only given precise numerical values in the main program before (or in) the orders which call for the use of the functions. It is most important to remember that the actual numerical values of the parameters must correspond in number, order and type with the dummy variables which they replace.

6.3 Subroutines

The use of functions in a program is somewhat limited. Each function can have only one set of parameters, which are used to calculate one quantity having the same name as the function itself. Often we need to perform more sophisticated calculations, needing more than one set of input parameters and calculating more than one output quantity. In these circumstances we introduce an extension of the idea of a function, called a subroutine. This differs from the function in that it can have more than one set of input parameters as its data and more than one output quantity as its results. Indeed a subroutine can be thought of as a complete program in its own right, subordinate to the main program, but differing from it only by being terminated by the order RETURN to return control to the main program, rather than the order STOP, which returns control from our main program to the central processor of the computer.

Thus, we might find it useful to have a way of removing the means from a set of data automatically. We have already written a complete program for doing this, which we can turn into a subroutine for general use quite simply.

```
SUBROUTINE MEAN (N, A)
DIMENSION A(100)
X = 0·0
Y = 0·0
DO 1 I = 1, N
```

$$Y = Y + 1{\cdot}0$$
$$1 \quad X = X + A(I)$$
$$DO\ 2\ I = 1,\ N$$
$$2 \quad A(I) = A(I) - (X/Y)$$
$$RETURN$$
$$END$$

In our master program, every time that we needed to remove the means from a sequence of N items held in $X(1)$, $X(2)$, – – – we would only need to write in the main program the order

$$DIMENSION\ X(100)$$

to define the size of the X sequence

and later on   CALL MEAN (N, X)

to call the actual subroutine, and the calculation would be carried out automatically. Note here that the sequence X must contain the actual data before the subroutine is obeyed. If we wanted to repeat the calculation with M items held in the sequence $Y(1)$, $Y(2)$, – – – we would simply write in our main program the orders

$$DIMENSION\ Y(100)$$
and later on   CALL MEAN (M, Y)

and these would perform exactly the same calculation using the parameters M and Y instead of N and X, that is to say, it would remove the means from the M items held in the sequence Y instead of from the N items held in the sequence X.

6.4 An example of a simple regression program

We are given a set of N observations of an event and each observation consists of a pair of numbers (X_i, Y_i). We wish to calculate the slope b, of the line

$$y - \bar{y} = b(x - \bar{x})$$

which minimizes the sums of the squares of the deviations parallel to the Y axis of the points (x_i, y_i) from this line.

A diagram will make the relations between the various quantities clearer. The usual formula for b, which is given in all elementary books on statistics, is:

$$b = \sum_{r=1}^{n} \{(y_r - \bar{y})(x_r - \bar{x})\} / \sum_{r=1}^{n} \{(x_r - \bar{x})^2\}$$

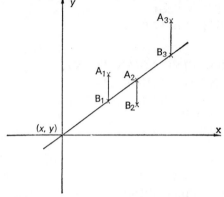

The flow chart is:

[Start]

(Read in N, and the N pairs of numbers (X_1, Y_1). $--$, (X_N, Y_N))

$\langle$Does N $= -1\rangle$ ➤ Yes ➤ [Stop]

No

[Form the means $\bar{x}$, $\bar{y}$]

[Remove the means from the data]

(Print the data with the means removed)

[Form the sums S $= \sum_{r=1}^{N} (y_r - \bar{y})(x_r - \bar{x})$ and T $= \sum_{r=1}^{N} (x_r - \bar{x})^2$]

(Print B $=$ S/T)

[Return to the start ready to read in another set of data]

We shall use a subroutine to remove the means from the data.
The full program with heading sequence is:

```
        PROGRAM (REGS)
        INPUT 1 = CRØ
        OUTPUT 2 = LPØ
        END

        SUBROUTINE MEAN (N, X)
        DIMENSION X(100)
C   REMOVE MEANS
        XBAR = 0·0
        XN = 0·0
        DO 11 I = 1,N
        XN = XN + 1·0
11      XBAR = XBAR + X(I)
        XBAR = XBAR /XN
        DO 12 I = 1, N
12      X(I) = X(I) − XBAR
13      FORMAT (8H MEAN = , F5·3)
        WRITE (2,13) XBAR
14      FORMAT (25H DATA WITH MEANS REMOVED.)
        WRITE (2,14)
15      FORMAT (10F5·3)
        WRITE (2,15) (X(I), I = 1,N)
        RETURN
        END

        MASTER REGS
        DIMENSION X(100), Y(100)
C   SIMPLE REGRESSION
C   READ DATA
1       FORMAT (I 2)
8       READ (1, 1) N
        IF (N + 1) 2, 2, 3
4       FORMAT (/11H END OF RUN)
2       WRITE (2, 4)
        STOP
3       READ (1, 5) (X(I), Y(I), I = 1, N)
```

```
5   FORMAT (2F5·2)
    CALL MEAN (N, X)
    CALL MEAN (N, Y)
    S = 0·0
    T = 0·0
    DO 6 I = 1, N
    S = S + X(I) * Y(I)
6   T = T + X(I) * X(I)
    B = S/T
7   FORMAT (/4HB = , F5·2)
    WRITE (2, 7) B
    GOTO 8
    END
    FINISH
```

The data consists of one card (or printed line) containing N
punched as a two-column integer, followed by N cards (or printed
lines) each containing an X followed by its Y. The X's and Y's are
punched as five-column numbers with the decimal point falling
in the third column of each field. The whole set of data is terminated by −1.

For example, our data might be:

8	
5·12	4·13
5·75	4·01
5·98	3·75
6·31	3·01
7·10	2·91
7·52	2·57
7·91	2·33
8·30	2·01
−1	

Exercises 6.2

1   Punch up this program, with its subroutine, heading sequence
    and data, either on paper tape or punched cards and test it
    on the computer.

2 Work out by hand the result you would expect from this data, and check it with the result from the computer.

3 Add sections to your program to carry out these further calculations on the same set of data:

Using the x data without the means removed print:

    (*i*) The largest value of x, x_{max}

    (*ii*) The smallest value of x, x_{min}

   (*iii*) The median, $\frac{1}{2}(x_{min} + x_{max})$

   (*iv*) The range, $x_{max}-x_{min}$

    (*v*) The frequency distribution, that is, the counts of the number of x's which fall into each of the ten equal intervals between x_{max} and x_{min}

   (*vi*) The variance, $v = \sum x^2/(N-1)$

  (*vii*) The standard deviation, $s = \sqrt{v}$

 (*viii*) The standard deviation of the mean, $s/\sqrt{N}$

   (*ix*) The coefficient of variance, $100s/\bar{x}$

    (*x*) Student's t, $= -\bar{x}\sqrt{N}/s$

   (*xi*) The mean square of successive differences

$$d = \sum_{i=1}^{N-1} (x_{i+1} - x_i)^2/(N-1)$$

Using the x data with the means removed,
if $dev_i = x_i - \bar{x}$, print:

    (*i*) The number of positive signs in the sequence dev_i

    (*ii*) The number of negative signs in the sequence dev_i

   (*iii*) The trend, $T = 12 \sum (dev_i)^2/(N^3 - N)$

   (*iv*) The standard deviation of the trend

$$S = \sqrt{\{12 \sum (dev_i)^2/(N^3 - N)\}}/(N-2)$$

    (*v*) T/S

   (*vi*) The mean deviation $\sum |dev_j|/N$

  (*vii*) The beta one statistic

$$[\sum (dev_i)^3/N]^2/[S^2(N-1)/N]^3$$

 (*viii*) The beta two statistic

$$[\sum (dev_i)^4/N]/[S^2(N-1)/N]^2$$

There are many other concepts in Fortran not mentioned here. There are logical variables which can take only the values 'True' or 'False'. There are double-length variables which we can use to do arithmetic on numbers which have up to twenty significant digits. There are special groups of orders to control magnetic tapes, disc files and other special equipment.

Since Fortran is a living language, created and used by human beings, it is constantly being improved and extended. As the student gains more experience in writing programs and using computers, he will be able to study these extra facilities as he needs them. This book contains all that will be required to make a good start.

Further reading

CALDERBANK, V. J., *A course on programming, Fortran IV*, Chapman & Hall, 1969.

FIELKER, D. S., *Topics from Mathematics, Computers*, Cambridge University Press, 1967.

GOLDEN, J. T., *Fortran IV, Programming and Computing*, Prentice-Hall, 1965.

JACOBOWITZ, H. and BASFORD, L., *Electronic Computing made simple*, W. H. Allen, 1967.

JAMISON, R. V., *Fortran Programming*, McGraw-Hill, 1966.

MCCRACKEN, D. D., *Fortran Programming*, John Wiley, 1963.

MURRAY-SHELLEY, R., *Computer Programming*, English University Press, 1967.

ORGANICH, E. I., *A Fortran IV primer*, Addison Wesley Press, 1968.

SLATER, L. J., *Fortran Programs for Economists*, Department of Applied Economics, Occasional Paper, No. 13, Cambridge University Press, 1968.

STEIN, K. L. and MUNRO, W. D., *A Fortran Introduction to Programming and Computers*, Academic Press, 1966.

WATTERS, J., *Fortran Programming*, Heinemann, 1968.

WELBOURNE, D., *Analogue Computing Methods*, Pergamon Press, 1965.

Index

Accumulators, 1
Addition, 3, 18
Algol, 11
Arithmetical statements, 14, 17
Auxiliary storage units, 8

Basic machine codes, 10
Brackets, 22
Built-in functions, 88

Card punches, 7
Card readers, 7
Check data, 53, 77
Clearing the store, 85
Compilers, 89
Continuation columns, 59
Continue orders, 69
Control, 11
Curve plotters, 9
Cycles, 33, 62, 68

Decimal formats, 41, 45
Decimal numbers, 18
Dimensioning sequences, 71
Disc files, 9
Division, 4, 21, 23
'Do' loops, 68

Equals signs, 17
Exponentation, 28

Floating point, 8
Flow diagrams, 12, 14, 16
Fortran, 11
Functions, 88, 91

Hardwear, 9
Heading sequences, 49
H formats, 56
High level programs, 10
Histograms, 37

'If' orders, 32
Initialization of the variables, 35
Input systems, 1, 5, 41
Integer formats, 47
Integers, 25

Jump orders, 30, 69

K as a measure of size, 2

Labels, 30
Lineprinters, 7
Lists, 45, 64
Logical statements, 30
Loops, 33, 68, 79

Magnetic tape, 8
Main stores, 2, 8
Means, 24, 55, 95, 98
Multiplication symbols, 20
Multipliers, 4

Named variables, 82
Nested loops, 75
Non-executable orders, 42

Orders, 14
Organizing programs, 10
Output systems, 7

Paper tape, 6
Parameters, 92
Power supplies, 1
Programming forms, 24
Punched cards, 6
Punching, 24

Regression program, 96
Repeated addition, 40
Return orders, 92

Sign digit, 4
Significant figures, 8
Softwear, 9
Solidus symbol, 21
Source programs, 11

Sprocket holes, 6
Square roots, 29, 89
Standard deviation, 90
Subroutines, 95
Subscripted variables, 64
Subtraction, 19
Systems programs, 9

Tape readers, 7
Teleprinters, 7
Terminating sequences, 49
Time sharing, 10

Variables, 64
Variance, 100